How to say when you feel you ought to say YES

Vera Peiffer works as an analytical hypnotherapist and health kinesiologist. She is an international speaker and runs workshops and courses in England, Germany and Italy. Vera is principal of the Peiffer Foundation, which is concerned with teaching practical life skills.

How to say NO when you feel you ought to say YES

How to Escape the Duty Trap

Vera Peiffer

ISBN 1-84333-056-3

A catalogue record for this book is available from the British Library

First published in 2002 by
Vega
64 Brewery Road
London, N7 9NT

A member of **Chrysalis** Books plc

Visit our website at www.chrysalisbooks.co.uk

Cover design, Grade Design Consultants, London
Printed in Great Britain by CPD, Wales

CONTENTS

A thing is not necessarily true because a man dies for it.

Oscar Wilde

INTRODUCTION

FATHERS WALKING out on their families, refusing to pay maintenance; old people in homes who are rarely visited by their offspring; small children left for days while their single mother goes off on holiday; pets abandoned by the roadside once they have lost their novelty value; there are reports of selfishness, cruelty and negligence in the media every day and we are appalled.

What we usually *don't* hear about is the other extreme – people with a sense of duty so strong that they damage or even destroy their physical and mental health. These cases are often hidden away from public view, and because general opinion has it that these people are 'only doing their duty' many feel that they don't merit any particular mention. It is significant that those who have a strong sense of commitment – people in the caring professions for example – are paid a pittance for their hard and responsible work, and that there are no adequate schemes available to enable those who care for disabled or handicapped relatives full-time to take sufficient time off to recharge their batteries.

Personal commitment, loyalty and responsible behaviour are just as important today as they have always been. These values are essential if we are to ensure good co-operation and a harmonious atmosphere between individuals and groups of people, be it in a private or in a professional environment.

However, there is also a need to understand that it is necessary to draw the line when physical or emotional wellbeing are jeopardized.

A great deal of misery is suffered every day by people behaving towards others out of a sense of duty. Unhappy marriages and relationships are kept together, even though they are beyond repair; unkindness is quietly tolerated by adult children who have never managed to detach themselves from the cruel parent; intolerable treatment at work is suffered, even at the expense of health and sanity. True to the teachings of the church, people live by the rule that they have no right to consider their own needs, but instead must devote themselves to the needs of others. Leaving an untenable situation therefore often becomes impossible because of a strong sense of guilt that accompanies even the mere thought of wanting to look after one's own happiness. It is the fear of being judged an uncaring and selfish person that makes people remain in an unhappy environment.

The Duty Trap is aimed at those men and women who find themselves trapped in an untenable life situation, but feel they are not allowed to make their own decision for fear of being judged unfavourably. The book looks at how we come by our concept of duty and how we can become ensnared in it, and at how others can manipulate us by developing and maintaining our feelings of guilt to ensure that we continue to consider their needs rather than our own.

The Duty Trap shows ways out of the dilemma which allow for dignified and responsible solutions to situations where duty has already become or is threatening to develop into a burden. In order to implement these solutions, a sense of self-esteem is essential. The book shows how to build self-reliance and esteem so that you are able to negotiate a better deal for yourself without being held back by feelings of guilt. If other people's happiness can only be achieved at the expense of your own, you have a responsibility towards yourself to re-negotiate your situation. Ultimately both decisions and their judgement rest with you and you alone.

Part I

DUTY AND ITS PITFALLS

1

HAS MODERN LIFE BECOME
A DUTY-FREE ZONE?

How OFTEN have you used the word 'duty' in conversation over the last few years? Chances are, hardly at all. 'Duty' sounds old-fashioned, self-righteous and a bit pompous, reminiscent of those days when men were required to do their duty for King and Country, when women were seen but not heard and couples stayed together because divorce was a practical and social impossibility.

But even though most people avoid using the term nowadays, the concept of duty is still very much with us on an emotional level. Every time we use the expression 'I should', we are referring to something we know would be right to do but which, for one reason or another, we cannot bring ourselves to do. 'The doctor told me to stop smoking, and I know I should, but ...'; 'I know I should fit a light to my pushbike now that it is getting darker in the evenings, but ...'; 'I know I should make more time to be with my children, but ...'.

When we become aware that there is something we ought to do because common sense dictates it or because others expect it of us, but we still don't do it, we feel some degree of emotional discomfort. Interestingly, this emotional discomfort, also known as guilty conscience, is not always sufficient to get us to do the task in question. Many people choose to suffer weeks of self-recrimination and unease rather than take an active step towards doing what they know will relieve their emotional burden.

As long as our avoidance behaviour concerns only ourselves, our failure to do 'the right thing' can be written off as either personal choice or folly. However, in most cases, our inability or unwillingness to implement an obvious solution to a problem will have negative repercussions on others around us, such as our parents, children, spouse, friends or colleagues at work. Someone who has had an incident of skin cancer but who still sits in the sun for hours on end may be said to precipitate his or her own death, but at the same time they are upsetting their family who have to watch helplessly as their words of warning are ignored. A person who has already been stopped for speeding does not only risk losing their licence if they continue to offend, but they also jeopardize their job if they need their car for work, and this could have serious implications on their family life – this is not to say that it is always easy to do the right thing. Even though we may know what we should do, the force of habit or fear of failure can stop us, as can the belief that it will be difficult or unpleasant to implement the positive change.

When you do something out of a sense of duty, it means that you are conforming to expectations which have been imposed on you from the outside. In this way you are required to act regardless of your own wishes and desires, so that an act of duty is usually regarded as an unpleasant chore. You may have had a gruelling week at work, and yet you feel you need to clean the house over the weekend, even though you would rather sit around and just relax. You may feel morally obliged to help someone, even though they have always treated you badly. If you followed your instincts you would leave them to their own devices, but you don't want to sink to their level, so you help them. You may stay in a bad marriage because you feel it is your duty to honour your vow of 'for better or for worse, 'til death us do part', no matter how depressed you feel and how unhappy the children become.

When you feel duty-bound to do something, your own

needs are being put on the backburner. As you live your life according to rules and regulations that have been made by others, you may be deemed a worthy and moral person by others, but there is a price to be paid for denying your own needs if you do so on a regular basis.

The problem is that it is often not clear where free will ends and duty begins. You may feel genuinely sorry for someone in distress and be quite prepared to help them out and do so over a period of time. You do so quite happily until your private life begins to suffer and you would like to extricate yourself from your voluntary work but feel trapped by the other person's expectations. They have come to rely on you, and as you realize their dependency on your help, it makes you feel bad about yourself every time you consider the possibility of restricting or even withdrawing your support. What has started as a human gesture has imperceptibly turned into a chore and a burden. As a consequence, your emotional (and often physical) wellbeing is affected, and often your relationship to the person you are helping changes. As frustration sets in, resentment builds up which you may or may not be able to prevent from showing.

Many people prefer not to get involved in the first place, maybe in anticipation of these complications. They may be aware of their moral duty to help their fellow man, but they have become (or have always been) too selfish to consider others. The attitude of 'looking after number one' can result from negative experiences in your past, where nobody helped you when you needed it. As a consequence, you had to fend for yourself, and this can make you hard towards others, regarding any requests for help as a regrettable weakness. 'Nobody ever helped me; why should others have it any easier?'

People who had to toughen up as children because they were not supported and encouraged by their parents often develop without enough emotional scope for altruism. Strangely enough, it is those children who were emotionally neglected who are the spoilt ones: they have been ruined because their fears were never assuaged, their self-doubts never quelled and their ability to cope with problems never furthered in a positive manner. They were thrown in at the deep end and left to struggle with life by themselves, so how on earth can they take anyone else's feelings into consideration later on in life? However, personality will also play a part in the development of a person. Some men and women have gone through very bad times as youngsters and still emerge as caring adults.

Modern legislation is often not on the side of those who want to help. At the moment it is possible that someone who comes to the aid of a street attack victim will end up in prison rather than the attacker if the assailant gets hurt.

In addition, the governmental screws are also tightened on the growing number of people with special needs, such as older people. With financial responsibilities being transferred from government to the local social services, some authorities who have a majority of older people find that their allocated funds are not sufficient to provide adequate service for all their elderly. Also, low pay, low prospects and low morale amongst nurses and carers lead to burn-out – one of the main reasons for the high incidence of mental and physical illness amongst carers.

In addition, the mainly negative selection of news items in the media does nothing to encourage people to take the initiative when assistance is required. Do you stop your car when a woman is lying by the side of the road, or do you drive on because it is getting dark and this might be a trap? Do you go over to check out what is the matter with the old man who is swaying across the common or do you just walk past quickly, worried that he might attack you? Would you let a stranger who says he needs to make an emergency phone call into your house, or would you say 'no' because you are afraid he has come to rob you?

There is no doubt that violence in the streets has increased. As the pace of life changes to a murderous tempo for those in high-pressure jobs and to a dead pace for others through unemployment, alcohol and other drugs become the artificial saviours of sanity, at least temporarily, until they engulf the person and become their master. Frustration and hopelessness complete a lethal cocktail of hate, aggression and violence, be it verbal or physical, which spills over and makes lurid newspaper headlines.

Good things happen too, but we don't seem to hear about them so much. It is not surprising that the overwhelmingly negative nature of news items creates an atmosphere of mistrust in many who would like to help but are afraid to do so for fear of becoming a victim themselves.

2

WHERE DO WE GET OUR SENSE
OF DUTY FROM?

THE CONCEPT of duty is an old and very powerful one,
strongly supported by churches and faiths of all denomi-
nations. We feel we 'owe' our parents, our employers, our
neighbours, our friends, but where did that feeling come
from originally? How did we arrive at this understanding
that certain tasks have to be carried out, irrespective of
whether we approve of them or not, whether we consider
them necessary, wise or useful?

CULTURE AND SOCIETY

When we are born, we enter a cultural heritage which
accompanies us throughout our life and continues after our
death. To a large extent, we are unaware of this cultural
backdrop and its profound influence on us.

Our everyday life is shaped by cultural traditions such as
our economic and political systems with all their associated rules and regulations. A credit card can only have a
meaning for someone who is part of a society which is
founded on a particular way of administering their finances;
such a card has no meaning to a tribe in a rain forest.
Similarly, the implications of a General Election can only
be understood within a particular political framework and

might therefore be quite bewildering to the proverbial man from Mars.

Our cultural heritage provides the framework for our lives, and supplies the values and beliefs which will determine the criteria of worth we allocate to abstract ideas and material objects. The culture we live in determines not only moral standards but also ways of evaluating performance generally. Our culture tells us what is good or bad, true or false, and these values and beliefs are so inextricably interwoven with everything we do that it is easy to forget that they are man-made and a product of past actions, rather than a law of nature.

Within our culture, it is our social system which imposes some order on the behaviour of individuals through the process of institutionalization. Cultural values and beliefs are represented in social institutions which establish rules and regulations concerning government, law, property and marriage, as well as prescribing rules that outline expectations about proper and acceptable behaviour. Each person in society, depending on his or her role, is expected to perform certain functions in ways that are considered to be appropriate. A mother is expected to look after her children; if she neglects to do so, the law courts will intervene. A bank manager is expected to manage other people's money; if instead he walks off with it, he is in violation of the law and will be prosecuted. Motorists are expected to be sober while driving, and if they are not, they can get into trouble. Social institutions lay down the law and define our duties, both on a practical and on a moral level.

Institutions such as marriage and the family are also governed by social norms. Over the last century, the family structure has changed, and with it the moral norms that guide it. Marriages today are no longer made out of moral, social or financial necessity, but out of love – a notion that would have been considered utterly decadent only 150 years ago. Whereas then incompatibility between partners would have been a cross to be borne in silence, it is now sufficient reason to dissolve the marriage.

We are now clearly and perhaps, irrevocably moving

away from the old family structure. We have left behind the extended family, and we are now in the process of leaving behind the traditional nuclear family. Partners are often not married, even if they have children together, and many couples decide not to have children at all. There is an increase in the number of single parents, not through death of a partner but through choice, and old people have no family because their children no longer live in their immediate vicinity. The working population has had to become more mobile in its search for employment which often results in family members living at a considerable distance from one another. In addition to being deprived of a well-established social network of colleagues, retired people also often lose the proximity of relatives once they have given up work.

The rules that govern a person's moral obligations today go back to a time when inequality between the sexes was the order of the day, where the teachings of the church dominated everyday life and where it was politically desirable if the man in the street unquestioningly gave his all to the state, both in times of peace and in war. Western society has moved on a long way since then, and moral values will need to move with the times before they become bulldozed down by indiscriminate striving for individual self-fulfilment. However, the only way old values can adapt to a changed society and survive into the 21st century is if they finally become officially embued with the concept of self-respect, rather than the one-sided burden of having to respect another person just because they are of a particular gender, of a professionally higher rank, of a greater age, or because they are a family member.

RELIGIOUS ASPECTS

Let us hear the conclusions of the whole matter:
Fear God, and keep his commandments:
for this is the whole duty of man.

Ecclesiastes 12:13

Religion is and always has been a universal phenomenon. Societies and religions have both existed since the dawn of mankind and have developed, diversified and changed from one century to the next.

For many hundreds of years, churches in the Western world held a dominant position in society. Bishops and cardinals were influential people, and popes were so powerful that they could threaten a king's position. When King Henry IV of Germany violated an agreement he had with the church and attempted to depose Pope Gregory VII, the Pope replied by excommunicating Henry and absolving his subjects from their oaths of allegiance which, in real terms, equalled dethronement. The only way Henry could ensure his position as King was to eat humble pie, go to Canossa and do penance before the Pope, which he did in 1077. He was consequently re-admitted to the church and remained king.

Today, the political influence of churches in the Western world has waned considerably. However, churches and religion still have an impact on public issues, on people's conduct and on their perception of the world. A lot of the church's influence dates back to the times when religion was conducted in a highly formalized way, with very strict and often narrow rules as to what was right or wrong. Only a hundred years ago, it would have been impossible for any self-respecting citizen to fail to attend mass on Sunday, for a couple to just live together rather than get married in church, or to disregard religious ceremonies such as a christening or baptism, holy communion, confirmation or barmitzvah (depending on which faith you subscribed to). Your church told you what to think, based on what the Bible prescribed. In some ways this made life easier; everyone went to church every Sunday and heard what was expected of them. Many of the commandments from the Old Testament have long since been adopted by the civil law courts. It is a criminal offence to kill, or to lie in certain situations. Also, Family Law stated until very recently that the act of adultery by one partner in marriage gives the other partner the right to a divorce.

The disadvantage of your guidelines being prescribed by the church (and this is still done today by some churches) was that because of the very literal interpretation of the Scriptures, the great majority of human lapses and many human needs were interpreted as sins, bringing shame and guilt onto a person. This 'fire and brimstone' exertion of conformity to divine law did not allow for any human weaknesses, nor any consideration of your circumstances or the conditions under which you failed. Being human already condemned you as a sinner. You could not fail and be forgiven. This meant that it must have been practically impossible not to commit at least one sin every day, and so it was quite easy for people to accept the label of 'sinner', especially because you were not allowed to question the authority of the Bible or that of the religious representatives of the church. That would have been yet another sin; only if you abdicated your free will could you be reasonably sure that you would go to Heaven after you died.

Today some churches have changed to a certain extent. With the recognition that it is impossible to comply with all the laws and commandments of the Bible all the time, some clergy have moved towards a more liberal interpretation of the Scriptures, which sees God as the loving father of mankind who values you and forgives your mistakes so that you in turn are enabled to value the world around you. The previously coerced compliance with religious laws is nowadays being given an extra dimension, namely that of self-determination. What was formerly interpreted as duty has now become a responsibility where circumstances can be taken into account and you are no longer compelled to bear the cross of, for example, an unsustainable relationship at all costs. You are also allowed to consider your own needs.

However, the official voice of most churches is still that of the traditional, strict interpretation of the Bible, and it is those old rules that appear to have been so thoroughly absorbed into people's minds that the messages are being passed on through the generations, even if people attend church services less frequently today.

3

VALUES WITH A DIFFERENCE

WITH A general relaxing of social and moral codes, many formerly clear boundaries have become blurred or totally redefined. Whereas before the Second World War, women tended to work while they were single and give up their jobs as soon as they got married, today women are found in nearly all job categories and, in some industrial areas, find it easier to secure work than the men who face long-term unemployment because traditional industries have disappeared.

The increasing involvement of women in professional life has also had an effect on the stability of marriages. While a hundred years ago it would have been impossible for most women to leave their husbands because they would not have been able to support themselves, this is frequently not the case today. Topics such as sex, contraception, abortion and abuse were unmentionable in the past, but can now be openly discussed and broadcast to the public.

All these changes might appear to indicate that society is disintegrating, with old values such as virtue, honesty and honourable behaviour being lost forever, but this is too hasty a conclusion to draw. The official moral codes may have been stricter in the past, with the church having the most important influence in determining what was right and what was wrong, but rules were broken then just as they are now. Because no one was allowed to speak about abuse does not mean it did not happen. Pre-marital and extra-marital sex were not sanctioned by the church but still happened – pregnant girls were left behind by dishonourable lovers and husbands cuckolded by faithless wives, now as then. That the church commended to their parishioners to love their neighbours did not mean that there was not argument, intrigue and malice. Even though official moral codes may have changed and the influence of the church on people's decisions and conduct has lessened, human nature has not changed; people's basic needs are still the same. They want to be liked and loved, they want approval and security, they want to be entertained and thrilled, and they want to lead a carefree life. The pursuit of happiness has always been and will always be there, and in attempting to find contentment, people will always encounter obstacles, make mistakes and suffer discouraging setbacks.

Just as human nature will always stay the same, essential values, such as honesty, loyalty, commitment and compassion, will remain the same, even though different generations may give them different names. However, one important change needs to be made to enable these old values to work in today's society – they need to be reciprocated between people.

RESPONSIBILITY

Whatever actions you take, whatever decisions you make in everyday life, the chances are that at least one other person besides you will be affected. If you decide to finish off a particular piece of work in the office, even though it is already late, your secretary may have to work overtime, or your spouse and children may miss out on your company. If you have problems with your partner and allow them to fester, your bad mood or irritability may affect your colleagues at work, or your children. Whether you make a decision or not, there are usually others to consider who become, directly or indirectly, part of a chain of events that you have set in motion. For this reason, it is essential that you think about the effects that your actions and decisions have on others: you have a duty of care towards them. These could be your children who you cannot simply leave behind without adequate supervision, just because you want to get away on a holiday by yourself. You also have a duty of care towards other road users, which means you cannot drive while you are drunk because you may hurt, maim or even kill another person. Your search for happiness and thrills needs to be reined in by a sense of responsibility towards others.

At the same time you have a duty of care towards yourself, which is just as important. It is not the fact that a single mother wants to have a holiday and get away from her children that is unacceptable – how many mothers haven't wished they could do so every once in a while? It is perfectly all right to acknowledge that you feel worn out and that you are in need of some peace and quiet. Contrary to public belief, it doesn't make you a bad mother because you want a break from your children, but it needs to be done in a responsible way.

When it comes to duty, the emphasis has always been on the individual's duty towards others, but this one-way-street morale needs to be balanced out to become liveable. You are equally responsible for your own wellbeing and happiness. In the past, the whole concept of duty relied on each individual doing their duty towards others, and that way, everyone was supposed to be seen to and looked after. Unfortunately, it does not work like that in real life. There are some people who do their duty, who are considerate and compassionate, and others who live off them, deliberately or unthinkingly. This is why your sense of duty towards others needs to be tempered by an acknowledgement of your own needs and wishes, and a willingness to take those needs as seriously as you take other people's. There is no point in blaming others for not doing their duty towards you or complaining about unfavourable circumstances that prevent you from achieving contentment.

Ultimately, the responsibility for your own peace of mind lies with you alone.

COMMITMENT AND LOYALTY

No job would ever get finished unless someone with a sense of commitment carried it through. This applies to all levels of tasks, from projects at work to relationships between individuals to relationships between nations.

The problem with promises that are given in all seriousness is that people often don't realize what they are letting themselves in for. The marriage vow may come from the heart at the time, but how is a young couple to know what it *really* means when they promise to stay together 'for better or for worse'? The good intention is there, but what if sudden unemployment or an inability to conceive starts putting long-term pressure on the relationship? What if one of the partners turns out to be entirely different to how they appeared before the marriage?

Promises need to be taken seriously and not abandoned as soon as the first difficulties set in. They have to be examined and discussed in order to find viable solutions, and this is where many professional and personal relationships fail. Non-communication by one or both parties allows a disruptive issue to fester over time, poisoning any goodwill and leading to distress and the corruption of what was once good. If one business partner feels that they have to shoulder more than their fair share of the workload, but will still do so without addressing the issue, commitment becomes undermined. If a grown-up daughter can never please her mother, no matter how hard she tries, this will jeopardize her commitment unless the matter is spoken about and sorted out. Even if you have committed yourself to a cause rather than a person, you may have to take time out to speak about those matters connected with the cause that are becoming a burden to you, or you risk getting emotionally overloaded and ultimately unable to honour your commitment.

When you have committed yourself to a task or a person, it is essential to do everything possible to make it work. You can only go if you have made a valiant effort to overcome the difficulties that make you want to quit. If a marriage is in trouble, your marriage vows oblige you both to do everything you can to sort out what is going wrong; it is not good enough to leave a note on the kitchen table. Walking out of a relationship just because you fancy another man or woman is dishonourable behaviour, as is a refusal to pay maintenance for your children, or making yourself unemployed to avoid paying. In the UK the Child Support Agency has not been a great success and has many serious shortcomings, but the underlying principle is certainly sound – when you make a commitment, you cannot just abdicate responsibility because you feel like it, even when you have very good reasons why you want to get out of the relationship.

However, it takes two to make any relationship work, be it between parent and child, husband and wife, girlfriend and boyfriend, employer and employee. Even though one partner may take their commitment to the relationship very seriously, the other one may not. Some parents assume that just because they are a parent they have only rights and no duties; some employers think that because they are the paymaster, they can expect loyalty from their staff, no matter how inconsiderate they are towards their employees. In cases such as these, commitment and loyalty have to be accompanied by common sense and honesty. Blind devotion and stubborn adherence to what you consider to be your duty is no substitute for being honest with yourself; you are simply hiding behind a smoke screen so that you do not have to look at something you would rather not see. It may be hurtful to admit to yourself that your father is a selfish person who is simply not interested in your wellbeing and just wants you to do your duty by him, just as it can be upsetting to realize that your boss has not an ounce of compassion when you get ill through an excessive workload which has been foisted on you, but it is better to face these facts earlier than later, before you are too exhausted or demoralized to deal with them in a constructive manner. This is not to suggest that you should change allegiance as soon as the going gets tough, but when you begin to feel uncomfortable and harassed a lot of the time you must start to examine *what* is going wrong, and *why*, so that you can look for ways out of the dilemma.

COMPASSION

Compassion is a valuable human quality, and those who are suffering can be greatly comforted by the knowledge that there is someone around who will spend time with them, listen to them or support them in any other way. People who have suffered a lot themselves often show a great capacity for empathy and a willingness to help, but as with commitment, compassion needs to be tempered with reason and balanced out with a certain amount of common sense.

All the great religions teach consideration and compassion for your fellow men. Christianity, Judaism and Islam ask their followers to either give part of their income to those who are in need or to feed anyone who is hungry and knocks on their door. In this way, those who have help those who don't have – an excellent thought in principle, which is taken up by millions of people who donate money each year to the many charities who support various good causes.

But, as the saying goes, charity starts at home, and this applies in a very real sense to many people who find themselves in a position where they have to or want to look after a severely handicapped member of the family, be it a retarded child or an old parent who needs round-the-clock attention. This can put immense physical, mental and emotional strain on the carer, no matter how much he or she loves the person they look after. Dementia renders old people irrational and confused and when the carer, after an exhausting day, is woken up in the middle of the night and asked to take the sufferer to the dentist because the old person believes they have an appointment, this can sorely try anyone's patience and empathy.

These are no doubt extreme cases, which would merit considerable practical support from the social services and this still needs to be brought to greater public attention so that the support is being made available. But even in less severe cases, it cannot be right that those who take upon themselves tasks out of a feeling of compassion are being ignored as 'just doing their duty'. A high percentage of women want to but also feel obliged to look after an ageing parent. This is fine as long as the carers don't forget about their responsibilities towards themselves. Compassion towards someone who is in need or frail needs to be counter-balanced with care towards oneself. If help is administered at the cost of one's own health and sanity, and if guilt stops you from adjusting the amount of help you give even though you are unwell yourself, you need to urgently check your motives or run the risk of destroying yourself.

4

WHERE TO DRAW THE LINE

THE DUTY of care needs to apply to both yourself and others if it is to be of real benefit. If the wellbeing of one person requires the sacrifice of someone else then one tragedy has simply been exchanged for another. I am not talking in this context about one-off emergencies where, for example, a father sees his little boy fall into a river and jumps in to rescue him. In these emergency situations, you have to act and be brave, and this could mean risking your own life. There is no time to think, and the desire to save one's own child is usually so strong that nothing else matters.

We are going to look at more everyday situations: mothers who have to cope with the dual task of working and looking after home and children; men and women who look after elderly relatives, part-time or full-time; young couples who are trying to build a life together but are not allowed to do so by interfering relatives, and so on. You want to help, you want to show you are grateful for what your parents have done for you in the past, you want to protect and nurture your children, but how far do you have to go? At what point are you allowed to stop and think of yourself? For some people, and especially women, the answer is never. Whenever they contemplate satisfying their own needs, they feel so guilty that they work even harder to make up for their 'selfish' thoughts. In the next two chapters, we will explore the reasons why people come to adopt these strong beliefs about their obligations.

So where do you draw the line? A good rule of thumb is probably to use any feelings of discomfort or unease as a sign to sit down and think about the situation. If you have taken on a duty which only very occasionally makes you feel annoyed, exhausted or bad-tempered, it is less important to take stock than if the task occupies your mind a lot of the time in a negative way. When your own needs get pushed into second place on a regular basis you must do something to improve the situation.

Here are a few questions you should ask yourself to see if you are beginning to lose control over the tasks you carry out as a matter of duty. Pick out one particular duty and check it against the following questions.

- Do you do the task cheerfully, but then feel negative afterwards?
- Do you do the task because you feel obliged for whatever reason, rather than wanting to do it?
- Do you spend a lot of time thinking about the task before and after you have carried it out?
- Do you dread having to do the task?
- Do you feel resentful having to do the task?
- Do you complain to others about having to do the task?
- Do you resent others not helping you with the task?
- Do you feel anxious before carrying out the task?
- Even though you are doing your best, do you still get criticized about how you carry out the task?
- Do you often feel angry after having done your duty?

If you answered 'yes' to even one of these questions, you have reached the point where it is time to sit down around the table with everyone concerned and have a constructive discussion or, if this is not possible, establish for yourself what it is you need from others to enable you to do the task more happily. You may also need to decide whether you want to make changes to the way in which you approach the task, or whether to abandon it altogether (see Part III).

Any regular task that you consider to be a duty has a tendency to take you over. Because it needs to be done at regular intervals, the task becomes a habit, and the way you think and feel about it becomes a habit too. After a while you become so used to getting annoyed or frustrated or exhausted when carrying out your duty that you forget that there was a time when things were better, and this is why it is important to stop every once in a while and test how you feel about carrying out that particular task.

Check Your Emotions Exercise

• Sit down and close your eyes.
• Listen to your breathing for a moment.
• Now tense all the muscles in your body, hold them to the slow count of five, and let them relax *very slowly*.
• Think about something really pleasant: an old memory that makes you feel good about yourself; an enjoyable encounter that has taken place recently; a person you like a lot. Check how your body feels and what thoughts are going through your mind.
• Now think about your task. Again, check how your body feels and what thoughts are going through your mind.

If you feel physically and emotionally comfortable while you recall your pleasant memory but uncomfortable when you think about your duty, something is out of alignment with regard to the task and you need to deal with it.

5

How Duty Can Become A Trap

COMMITMENT, LOYALTY and a sense of responsibility towards others are vital if living with other people is to be an ultimately rewarding experience for everybody involved. But commitment needs to come from both parties, not just from one side. When one person only gives and the other person only takes, the relationship is doomed. Think about human beings possessing a two-container mechanism in their emotional make-up – one container is for affection going out, the other for affection coming in. The two containers work in close conjunction and function most efficiently when both are full. The more love you have, the more love you can give. In order to give, however, you also need to receive. If you go for a long time without replenishing your resources, it becomes increasingly difficult to give. Remember the last time you were madly in love and your feelings were reciprocated? The world becomes a different place; you walk on air, you can do anything, you are happy, friendly and generous, and things that bothered you in the past become trivialities. Naturally, we cannot be in love all the time, but it shows what can happen when we have a maximum influx of affection. The happier you are, the happier you can make others. It has nothing to do with conditional love if you want commitment and loyalty from a person you are giving commitment and loyalty to. It is simply a function of the human emotional apparatus which will only keep going if it gets refilled regularly. When you find that you are giving commitment while you are left to run on empty, you know that you have got caught in the duty trap.

EXAMPLE
Simon was always there for his parents. Whenever they needed help with errands or with any repairs in the house, Simon would be the first to offer help. He even changed his private plans sometimes to make sure his parents' needs could be accommodated. However, when Simon needed a favour after his girlfriend had thrown him out of their shared flat, his parents refused to let him come and stay with them while he found himself a new place. Their reasoning was that they were used to having the house to themselves. Simon had to stay with a friend, even though his parents had a spare bedroom.

NEGLECTING YOUR OWN NEEDS

Performing what you perceive to be your duty is often done automatically. The attitude is that it has to be done and that there is no use thinking about it.

Some people feel a strong conviction that the duty *must* be done, no matter how inconvenient or unrewarding it is to them. The mere thought of decreasing their commitment evokes such strong feelings of guilt that, no matter how arduous the task, the person continues with their duty. In this way the guilt-barrier prevents the person from reaching down to those innermost emotions which are concerned with their own needs.

And yet you are never really safe from the feelings you are trying to ignore. Your own needs won't go away just because you refuse to look at them. There is really no point in sacrificing yourself at the altar of duty, because when you dislike doing what you are doing, it will show. It may show directly or indirectly, *but it will show*. You may come across as tense or moody, or you may be short and a bit impatient with the person who is at the receiving end of your efforts. For a moment, look at it from their point of view – would you like someone to do you favours when you know it is causing them great inconvenience? Would you like to be looked after by someone who looks or acts harassed? Probably not.

Even if you are good at hiding it, your stress will still manifest itself in your body or mind sooner or later. Suppressed emotions are a time bomb ticking away inside you. Sleepless nights, tiredness, migraines, high blood pressure and even panic attacks, phobias, obsessive-compulsive disorders (checking and rechecking locks, taps and so on) and depression can frequently be traced back to the suppression of needs and wishes.

If you do something out of a sense of duty, you act on expectations that are foisted on you by the outside world in general or by a specific person in particular, and over the years you take those expectations on board. You may have rebelled against them at first, but the subtle and continuous drip-feeding of guilt whenever you didn't comply to these expectations begins to take its toll after a while – your feelings of guilt make you override your own needs and wishes. Now you are trapped because the guilt triggers your compliance reliably every time duty beckons, until you cannot even remember that you ever had any needs of your own.

Often, there is an expectation that you would be rejected or rebuked by the recipient of your care if you were to mention your own needs. In some cases this expectation is based on past experience, but sometimes this fear is quite unnecessary, and by not dealing with the matter, you are prolonging your agony for no good reason. The easiest way to assess the likelihood that the other person will be sympathetic is to think back and check what you know about him or her. Have they generally proved to be understanding and caring themselves? If the answer is 'yes', you should certainly raise the issue of your own needs with them. There is more about how to do this in an acceptable way in Part III.

EXAMPLE
Hayley was the eldest of three children and the only girl.
Her mother, a discontented and frequently bad-tempered
woman, made her do all the cleaning in the house. The
boys were not required to help at all. Hayley was angry
at this unfairness but did not dare rebel too often as she
realized early on that her mother's approval, limited though
it was, was entirely dependent on Hayley complying with
her mother's demands. As an adult, Hayley became very
anxious whenever she hadn't tidied up her own home. She
felt guilty, and even though her mother no longer told her
what to do, Hayley had internalized her 'duty' and wiped
out her own needs.

FEELING OBLIGED

Another reason that keeps people carrying on with an unpleasant duty is because they feel obliged to someone else. Maybe
that person has done them a big favour in the past, or maybe
the dutiful person feels indebted in some other way. Whereas
it is laudable to want to show your gratitude, there is no need
to put lifelong pressure on yourself to perform the impossible
just to demonstrate your appreciation over and over again.

It goes without saying that one good deed deserves another.
When a friend was there for you when your relationship broke
up and he is now in the same situation, it is only right that you
help him. There is a bond between real friends that makes
them *want* to help one another; there is no obligation involved.
You like your friend, you respect him for his qualities, you like
to spend time with him and you are concerned when he has a
problem. Consequently, your natural impulse is to help him to
the best of your ability when he goes through a rough patch.

Sometimes all you can do is listen and give people a shoulder
to cry on; sometimes you are able to ask them to stay with
you for a while until they get over the worst; sometimes
you can assist them financially. The degree to which you

are able to help will vary, and the emphasis is not on the actual way in which you help but rather on the fact that you are *happy* to help as best you can. You may be unable to support your friend financially, but if the relationship is based on warmth and understanding they will accept that. 'Obligation' is irrelevant between really good friends. You may have experienced this yourself over such simple matters as visiting friends or relatives. You know that you have a good relationship with someone when you feel free to go to bed early if you are tired, and you can do so without a guilty conscience because you know your friends will accept your decision. You may feel less at ease with other people, and therefore less inclined to give in to your own needs; instead, you would feel obliged to 'stick it out', even though you can hardly keep your eyes open.

Some people will perpetuate your indebtedness to them by repeatedly referring to what they have done for you in the past ('How can you be so ungrateful after all that I've done for you?'). They are indirectly telling you that they want a return on their investment and that you will have to oblige them now to remain in their good books. People who use this type of emotional blackmail usually come from a family where co-operation was exerted rather than encouraged, and consequently, whatever they did for *you* in the past, they felt they *had* to do. And now they expect you to buckle down and do your duty by them. It is irrelevant whether you do it willingly or not; all that counts is that you do it. They never liked doing their duty, so why should they care that you don't like doing yours?

This is very much the old school of thought: duty is done without regard to your own person, and the greater the personal sacrifice you had to make in the course of duty, the more admirable and honourable you were deemed to be. This type of robot-like obedience to rules made by someone else is most strongly developed in the military, where you are given a medal or a memorial the less you care for your own and your men's safety and wellbeing. Unfortunately, neither a medal nor a commendation is of relevance when you have to spend the rest of your life as a physical or emotional cripple as a consequence of your adherence to your military duty. Your heroism is soon forgotten, and you are left to pick up the pieces, usually with very little support from a state you were prepared to sacrifice your life for.

EXAMPLE
Sabina had been brought up by her uncle and aunt after her parents were both killed in a car accident. She was clothed and fed with the couple's other children, but otherwise treated like an outsider. The uncle and aunt would throw a big party for their children's birthdays; Sabina's birthday was all but forgotten. The other children received expensive trips abroad as reward for passing their A-levels; Sabina received nothing. When Sabina decided to move out at the age of seventeen, she was called selfish and accused of being ungrateful for all that her uncle and aunt had done for her over the years.

FEARING DISAPPROVAL

In some relationships it is quite clear that there is an imbalance between giving and taking and even the person who is doing all the giving can see it. So why don't they simply refuse to give any more? Why can't they extricate themselves from an obviously untenable situation? The answer is that they are afraid that others might think them callous or irresponsible, or a horrible person. They are afraid that others would disapprove of them and lose respect for them for not persevering.

EXAMPLE
Emma is a single woman who lives close to her elderly mother. The mother is very demanding and expects Emma

to be at her beck and call. She is charming to everyone else and is generally regarded as a delightful old lady by neighbours and shopkeepers. But this is not how she is with Emma. Behind closed doors the mother complains, criticizes and is negative about anything her daughter says or does, but Emma still keeps coming, takes her mother out, ferries her to the doctor and supports her financially. The mother makes sure that Emma keeps doing this by telling her that other daughters look after their mothers much better, and how she, Emma, is the only one who is not really pulling her weight. Frequent rows ensue, but Emma keeps looking after her mother as she always has done.

Just thinking about having to see her mother makes Emma tremble visibly, but still she goes. Because how can she not go? All her relatives tell her that because she is the single one in the family it is only natural for her to see to mother's needs, and while she does so, they stay at a safe distance, away from mother's temper tantrums. Nobody would understand if she rebelled and refused to go on. Her brother and sister are both married with children, so they obviously cannot help, and it is true that she *is* single . . . . And her mother's neighbours and friends would certainly not understand because mother is so nice to them. They would be horrified to hear that the daughter wanted to have more time to herself; they would consider her cruel and heartless to abandon her old mother. The good-daughter image can only continue while the daughter is *seen* to perform her duty. If she slackens in her efforts, she runs the risk of being labelled 'selfish'.

But what about the mother's unacceptable behaviour? Does old age really entitle you to be rude and inconsiderate to your children? For that matter, does a professional position of authority entitle you to exploit people who work for you?

Working late in the office every day of the week and often also on weekends is fine for a while, especially if it is your own business. Hopefully, you will have planned carefully and things work out reasonably well so that you can relax a bit more once the business is up and running. However, problems start if you work long hours all week and even at weekends because someone insists you do more work than is reasonable for one person. This exhausting schedule can at times lead to confusion about the cause. If you lacked confidence when you started the job, you can end up feeling that your own inadequacy makes the long hours necessary. Even if you can see clearly that you are being given far too much to do, you might hesitate. Can you really afford to leave? Shouldn't you be grateful to have a job when so many people are unemployed?

When you spend a lot of time with a very demanding person who has unreasonable expectations of you, a certain negative brain-washing effect inevitably sets in. When your competence and willingness to help or to perform are continually questioned, you begin to doubt yourself, so that your confidence and self-esteem are not only undermined by the other person but also by yourself. The less self-confidence you have, the harder you feel you have to try to oblige, so you dig yourself deeper into a hole.

SECONDARY GAIN IF YOU STAY IN THE TRAP

One might think that being trapped in an inconvenient situation would automatically result in vigorous efforts to free oneself and gain greater comfort, but this is not necessarily so. Staying in the trap has distinct advantages for some people.

Perceiving a task as your duty means you know exactly where you stand. You may not have devised the rules upon which you act, but you are grateful to be given clear directives. At least you don't have to take responsibility if anything goes wrong because you were only obeying orders.

The extent to which human beings will subject their common sense and independent thinking to someone who they perceive to be in authority was demonstrated in the Milgram experiment which was carried out in the United States in the early 1960s. Volunteers were told that they were taking part in a study that examined the effect of punishment on learning. They were asked to punish another subject by giving them electric shocks whenever they made a mistake. The volunteers were told that the shocks were painful, but had no lasting damaging effect. Although the volunteers heard agonized cries from the victim, who was supposedly next door, 26 out of 40 subjects delivered the most intense shock possible which was clearly marked on the shock generator from 'mild shock' to 'danger – severe shock'. Some volunteers, on hearing the victim cry and bang against the wall (which was actually only a tape recording) turned to the experimenter to ask for guidance, but when he told them to continue, they did so. When Milgram spoke to the volunteers afterwards, they confirmed that they had been in distress over their actions, but more than half of them had nevertheless followed the instructions of the white-coated experimenter.

It is so much easier to obey orders than to oppose them. Being told what to do can feel quite safe because it allows you to abdicate responsibility for your actions. You can blame everything that goes wrong on whoever made the rules.

George Bernard Shaw said that when a stupid man is doing something he is ashamed of, he always declares that it is his duty. When you are frustrated with your marriage and you give your children a hard time instead of sorting things out with your partner, you can say that it is your duty as a parent to instil respect in your children. If you are afraid of emotional commitment to a relationship, you can hide behind your duties at work. And you know that nobody can get at you because you are only following officially sanctioned rules. So whenever something crops up that you don't want to do, you are using duty as an excuse to bow out. A friend invites you to attend an evening class with her but you decline. You are not sure whether you can handle learning something new, but instead of admitting this, you pretend that you could not possibly neglect your husband and children by going out in the evening . . .

Then there are those who enjoy the attention they get while they are suffering. These people are quite easy to make out because they will take every opportunity to tell you how they are suffering and why. Invariably, the cause of their anguish is attributed to them doing a lot for others and others not repaying their kindness. These martyrs will tell anyone who will listen how they are being taken advantage of, and they are happiest when they have an audience of sympathetic listeners. These tales of ingratitude are usually supplemented with stories of self-sacrifice and devotion on the part of the narrator, so that the martyr has finally proved that they are definitely right and the others are definitely wrong. If anyone dares probe into *why* the martyr is being treated in such an apparently appalling way and whether the martyr is possibly bringing it onto themselves by their own behaviour, the enquirer often meets with hostility and is accused of callousness.

This self-sacrificing attitude which demands approval from others reveals a belief in the nobility of suffering. True to the teachings of the church, human beings have no right to expect happiness during their life on earth. Instead they are required to wait until life after death where they will be rewarded for life's hardships. Bearing unhappiness thus becomes not just a duty but is, at the same time, elevated to a virtue.

EXAMPLE
Simone was exasperated with her 75-year-old father who was in bad health but still insisted on walking their large dog twice a day on the local common. Simone was very worried because their dog could get quite aggressive with other dogs, and there was a real danger of her father being knocked over and hurting himself. Simone took the dog out twice a day herself, before she went to work and when she came home in the evening. In the end, she found out that there was a very pleasant secondary gain to her father's daily excursions – it was a certain 70-year-old lady he had met on the common . . .

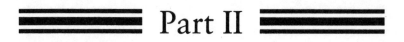

Part II

WHAT'S LOVE GOT TO DO WITH IT?

6

NOBODY IS AN ISLAND

ONE REASON why the concept of duty can seem elusive at times is that it is so deeply embedded in our cultural heritage that we are no longer aware how we came by our feelings of responsibility and obligation. Some rules and regulations governing our behaviour exist in writing in the form of laws, but other demands that are made on us are far less tangible. What is vaguely felt to be a moral obligation often does not exist as a secular law, but is passed on by example or through verbal instruction from one individual to another, usually from parents to children, and this is where emotions and personalities come into play.

UNDERSTANDING DEPENDENCY AND FAMILY TIES

When a baby is born, it is helpless and entirely dependent on physical and emotional support. If this support is insufficient the child becomes weak and, at worst, dies.

Very young children who have not yet learned to speak have a very straightforward way of communicating. If anything is wrong, if they are in pain, uncomfortable, frightened or hungry, they cry. This simple way of expressing their needs is usually followed by the mother's response of putting right what has been wrong – nappies get changed, the baby is fed or picked up and the appropriate action taken to ensure that the baby's needs are met.

As the baby gets bigger, he learns to walk and speak, but above all, he learns *not* to do things, especially those things that promise to be the most fun, such as sticking stones or beetles in his mouth, pulling the cat's tail or pouring green washing-up liquid all over the carpet. Also, he no longer receives so much sympathy when he cries, and adults make him say 'please' and 'thank you' if he wants something. As you get bigger, your parents as well as other adults expect more from you. All the early perks of being a young child are gradually withdrawn, and you are now expected to make an effort to fit in with the adults if you want their approval. The way you learn how to do this is quite simple: if you get it wrong someone will tell you off and call you 'naughty', and if you get it right, you get a smile and a pat on the head.

But even though the signals that teach you right from wrong are clear, the process of adapting to others around you is not an easy one. Children are still in direct touch with their feelings and needs and will attempt to have those needs fulfilled, not because they are unpleasant little creatures, but because this is a normal developmental stage. Consequently, it takes a lot of living and learning to let go of the self-centred phase and move on to a more mature balance of self-interest versus altruism.

A lot of what we have internalized as our duty comes from what we have been told by parents and other adults when we were children, and a lot comes from what we have observed in adults during our childhood and adolescence. As children, we notice how our parents deal with their responsibilities towards us, how they react when a neighbour is in need of help, and we observe how they deal with matters when *their* parents are getting old and dependent. Do our parents openly show displeasure at having to visit their parents? Do they make clear that it is a chore, or do they seem on genuinely good terms with their parents? Are there frequent rows before, during or after seeing the grandparents, or do parents slip into a different, artificial persona every time they go to visit? Children quickly register reluctance or unwillingness, even if it is not openly expressed, and it makes an impression on them.

One determining factor of how we will treat others is how we have been treated ourselves; the other factor is our personality make-up. If you were treated with love and respect, you are more likely to love and respect others. If, however, your childhood was dominated by an absence of warmth, by harsh criticism or even physical or verbal abuse, then these experiences will set the tone for what is to come. This does not necessarily mean that you will treat your parents or other people in the same way, but there is less likelihood of you *wanting*, for example, to help your parents when they are old. The charity Age Concern reports that physical, psychological and even sexual abuse of the elderly is not as uncommon as we might like to think. For children who have suffered parental abuse, abusing their parents or other old people later can be a form of revenge.

EMOTIONAL BATTLEFIELDS

In order to be accepted by others as a good and worthy person, you need to be seen to fit in more or less with what they expect of you. These expectations will vary and will depend (amongst other things) on your age, your gender, your role in life and your status in society. However, there are several specific transitional periods in each person's life cycle where problems are most likely to occur, and it is during those times when an individual changes their role or adds another role to an existing one.

Today, we understand that stress results when a family has difficulties getting past a particular stage in the life cycle. For example, a woman who is developing panic attacks after she has had her first baby may be struggling with the realization that her husband is showing no interest in the baby and is not helping at all, and that she therefore has to take all responsibility for the child herself, which means a serious or complete curtailment of her own personal needs. The life cycle has become stuck because the husband has not adapted to being a father.

There are five main stages of the life cycle: becoming an adult; moving in together or marriage; bringing up children; children leaving; and retirement. In connection with the issue of duty, it is the first four stages that I would like to look at briefly.

Many of the major dilemmas in life appear during the period when a youngster is developing into an adult. What happens during that time is crucial to the personal growth of the young person.

Young people who have reached late adolescence are expected to behave more responsibly and the adult members of the family cease to be tolerant if this development is not forthcoming. Being accepted as an adult now becomes clearly dependent on behaving like one. During this transition period, it also becomes important to establish a relationship; whoever does not manage to do so becomes an outsider. There is an age period, fortunately quite a long one, where young people are learning and experiencing how to deal with a potential future partner. The longer this process is delayed, either by parents who will not permit it, or by personality factors within the adolescent him or herself, the more likely it is that the adolescent becomes an outsider as an adult.

An adult-to-be needs to deal with his family and with his peers at the same time, and both groups make different demands on him. To help this development to unfold successfully, the adolescent must be allowed to wean himself gradually off his family while learning how to establish roots within an outside relationship and thus achieve independence and maturity.

Once a couple has moved in together their relationship changes, with each partner having to adapt to a new role and new responsibilities. Whereas they may have been seeing each other regularly and even stayed at each other's places, living together adds a new dimension to the relationship, and not everyone is prepared for the consequences. Whereas before everyone had their own private sphere, the living space now has to be shared and the partners have to negotiate situations which simply never arose. Can wet towels be left on the bed? Who does the washing-up? Do all social visits have to be made as a couple, or is it OK to go by yourself?

Moving in together is a public statement and even more so when accompanied by a marriage ceremony. In many ways marriage is a helpful rite of passage, because it highlights the need to make a shift to new ways of relating to one another, not just for the couple, but also for their respective parents.

With the birth of the first child, many of the arrangements that the couple have made need to be revised yet again. The relationship now extends from two people to three. Whereas for some couples expecting and having their first baby can be a wonderful time, others may struggle. If there have been cracks in the relationship before the pregnancy, it may now become more difficult to split up. This can lead later on to the child being made the scapegoat who takes the blame for unresolved marital problems. Once this child tries to leave home, a crisis arises because the parents have to face each other.

Once children arrive, interference from relatives and in-laws can become a problem. This can range from rows over what name to give the child to which kind of education it should receive. And this is on top of the parents disagreeing about the same issues!

In the same way as babies have to be weaned off their mothers, so mothers (and fathers) have to be weaned off their children once they are ready to go. While they have been bringing them up, a couple will have got used to a certain routine which accommodated the presence of their children. When the children leave, there is a vacuum which needs to be filled. Ideally, the couple will have cultivated other interests while the children were growing up, but in some cases, parents (and in particular mothers) have lived for their children to the exclusion of everything else. Children are sometimes used as vehicles for fulfilling dreams that parents would have liked to achieve for themselves but could not; therefore the child has to do it for them and, ideally, be immensely grateful to the parent in question. However, this sort of pressure is often considered unacceptable by children and so they cannot wait to get away from home, only to be told, 'After everything I have done for you!' This emotional blackmail will make some children feel guilty and stay at home, but others will be even more eager to leave, and sometimes cut off contact altogether.

Quite apart from the demands that developmental life-changes make on people's ability to adapt and take on board new responsibilities, there are also those situations where personality clashes make for volatile relationships so that it can become practically impossible to work or live in harmony. This can be particularly harrowing if one of the participants is required to carry out a duty which involves the other person.

Personalities can be at odds in a professional environment as well as in your private life. Just because you are members of the same family does not necessarily mean that you will get on.

Personality conflicts can arise for two main reasons. For one, there is the shared history between two people. If we take as an example the parent–child relationship, the events of the shared first fifteen or twenty years can often decide what will happen once the parent is old and weak and the child is the 'stronger' party. The relationship may have gone through an early phase where the parent was unduly strict, critical or even rejecting, causing hurt and a loss of self-esteem in the child. As the parent mellows in later years, the formerly critical attitude may well turn to praise and admiration for the child's achievements, but this often comes too late. The now grown-up child thinks, 'Yes, I *am* doing well, but not thanks to *you*! I needed your support then, not now!' Even though these words may never be said out loud, they nevertheless may determine the actions of the child once the parent is old and needs support.

The second conflict area between individuals is a distinct feeling of dislike for another person which is not always rooted in shared history. It may be a person's mannerisms, gestures or looks that will result in their hostile reception by others, or it may just be the chemistry between two people. We have all been in situations where we have felt 'drawn' to a person, either sexually or just in a friendly way. We say that we 'clicked' with that person immediately, or that we felt we had known them for a long time even though we have only just met them, and as a consequence, a firm friendship is established from day one. These soul-mate encounters are rare and, luckily, so are the dislike-at-first-sight situations, but when they happen, they can make life a misery for at least one of the couple who may find themselves forced to live or work together. Sadly, it has to be said that this type of dislike can also occur in families, usually resulting in a parent making one child an outsider in more or less subtle ways. Some children are treated more harshly because of their gender or because they look like a grandparent who a parent never got on with; perhaps one child might prove to be more headstrong than her siblings and therefore gets into trouble with parents who feel they cannot cope.

Whatever the reason why two people are at loggerheads, the quality of a relationship will have a direct impact on the willingness of either of them to help out the other. Feelings of reluctance and stubbornness can stand in the way of a charitable gesture where this would be an appropriate act. In this context, building up confidence and self-esteem with outside help, such as through therapy or counselling, can be very useful because it is only a confident person who can make a clear decision whether to cut themselves off or whether to attempt to negotiate a better deal (see p.119) with the person with whom they are having problems.

7

WHY LOVE WITHOUT BOUNDARIES WON'T WORK

RELATIONSHIPS BETWEEN human beings are ruled by emotions, even though these may never be expressed openly. In the workplace, there is theoretically no room for feelings; working people are expected to conduct themselves in a professional and neutral manner, focusing on the project in hand and not on personal or interpersonal matters. The reality, as we all know, is quite different. Company politics can cause considerable stress, and interpersonal wranglings often jeopardize the successful completion of projects. It is now being recognized, albeit slowly, that the zest with which people dedicate themselves to their work is largely dependent on the company's willingness to consider their employees' emotional welfare. We now also understand that absenteeism and loss of man-hours through stress-related illness can be reduced considerably by furthering better communication and by working on problem areas rather than ignoring them.

Similar power struggles can exist inside families, but whereas at work a semblance of professionalism is usually attempted, in the private home pretences are dropped. This may never become apparent to the outside world, as the family often closes ranks when others are looking on. However, the story can be quite a different one behind closed doors – the husband who entertains everyone at a party turns into a morose misanthropist; the kindly lady who takes food to her sick neighbour, emotionally neglects her own children.

When we are expected (or expect ourselves) to carry out a task as a matter of duty, we are supposed to disregard our own feelings. The degree to which you achieve this is then taken as a measure of your worthiness as a person. So if you *really* love your mother, you must not mind giving up your own life to make hers comfortable, and if you are *really* dedicated to your job, you must not resent ruining your health in the process of achieving targets.

But feelings come into everything we do, whether we want them to or not, so we might as well take them seriously.

WHAT HAPPENS WHEN BOUNDARIES ARE NOT RESPECTED

Emotions can sometimes get in the way when you need to assess a situation objectively, but they also have their advantages; the way you feel is a gauge that provides you with feedback about your own needs. But this ability to experience your feelings and acknowledge your needs is dependent on how adults reacted to you as a child.

As discussed earlier (p.35), very small children can and will voice their needs quite clearly. When a baby is hungry, she cries and consequently gets fed. When a small child is afraid at night, she cries or calls for her parents and is consequently reassured. But sometimes parents decide, for whatever reason, that it is unnecessary to reassure an anxious child. They may feel that the child is being obnoxious, difficult or over-sensitive by displaying her fear, and they punish her for being, as they see it, a nuisance. In families where there are continual rows between the parents, children become upset and anxious that one of the parents might leave. Many parents are so wrapped up in their own problems that they cannot see how the domestic upheaval affects the children, who are often too shy to voice their own feelings for fear of upsetting the apple-cart even more.

Once you have learned to believe that expressing your feelings is undesirable, you begin to push them away as best you can. Every time you ignore a feeling, you are giving away a bit more control. Your parents overrode your feelings, and you continue the tradition and deprive yourself of an opportunity to create a boundary around yourself for self-protection. As an adult, without the ability to acknowledge your feelings, and especially the so-called 'negative' feelings like anger, you are like a turtle without a shell – vulnerable to anything and anyone who wants to have a stab. Once you have been poked and hurt a few times you get so frustrated that you either lash out at random or withdraw and get depressed. If only you could allow yourself to feel the anger when it is still small and then use it constructively to tell people where they cannot trespass onto your territory any more, all the later hurt could be avoided. But by that time, you are so well trained in ignoring your emotions that you are no longer aware when someone oversteps the mark. All you are aware of is that you are suddenly in a bad mood, but you don't know why. And even when you have the courage to acknowledge that you have been upset by a hurtful remark, for example, you are likely to discredit your hurt by doubting its validity, just because this is what you have learned to do with your feelings. You have finally arrived at the conclusion that everyone else's feelings are more important then your own.

EXAMPLE
Fiona (46) is married with three teenage children. When the children arrived, she gave up her job because she did not like the idea of someone else looking after them. Her husband John was a good provider, but he had a tendency to regard women as second-class citizens, and here he was, stuck with four of them! Even though he was not disdainful in an open manner, he demonstrated nevertheless that he expected to get priority treatment. He would also frequently belittle Fiona in a jokey way and dismiss her opinions out of hand,

so that she began to keep them to herself. Family life was peaceful, but only as long as everyone did as John said.

For a long time, Fiona had felt unhappy in her relationship with John. She was aware that he was putting her down, but because he normally did it in a jovial way, she was never quite sure whether she was over-reacting. Fiona had been comfort eating for years, and it was only when she started therapy for her eating disorder that the marital problems began to emerge as a cause. When Fiona learned to take her own needs seriously and successfully negotiated with John to stop the put-downs, her eating habits went back to normal.

EVERY RELATIONSHIP IS AS GOOD AS ITS NEGOTIATED RULES

If you are lucky, you are surrounded by people who like and appreciate you and who are capable of communicating with you in a constructive manner when problems need to be resolved. When this is not the case and others treat you like a child, or try to foist their opinions and views onto you without acknowledging your own, you need to be able to stand your ground.

When you live or work with someone, your interactions with the other person are ruled by assumptions and understandings that are very often tacit. In a work environment, you will have signed a contract which specifies which tasks are your responsibility, but beyond these requirements the office rules which govern the interrelationship between staff are implicit rather than explicit. A lot will now depend on how compatible you are with the others at work. If you enter an office culture that thrives on gossip and you quite enjoy that yourself, you may very well feel at home there. However, if you find gossip distasteful, you will be in a quandry; you want to belong, but you don't want to be party to the mud-slinging that is going on around you. You now have the choice of either pretending that you are 'one of them' and go along with the gossip, or you can establish some kind of passive resistance where you listen to their talking behind other people's backs, but without adding to it yourself. Neither of these options is really satisfactory, because you end up in each case with a head buzzing with negative prattle and a feeling of revulsion at the end of the day. You may also begin to lose self-respect for your conniving with something that goes against the grain. The only way out of the dilemma is to make clear that you do not wish to be part of the backstabbing and you do not want to listen to it either, but this can be a scary prospect. What will the consequences be? Will you make yourself an outsider? Will *you* now become the butt of their gossip? In most cases your worst fears turn out to be unfounded, but sometimes the only solution is to look for another job.

When you are at odds with people in your own family, you don't have that luxury of exchanging them for a better set of relatives, so it becomes even more important to negotiate a set of rules that will take into account the needs of each family member. If you feel that your needs have been overlooked in the past, it is up to you to bring this to the attention of the others. If you never say anything, nobody will know that you are discontented. Other people cannot read your mind, even if they have known you for many years.

You may have to be persistent in the negotiating process because old ways of doing things in a family often don't change that easily. People tend to relapse into old patterns in certain trigger situations, so you have to be on your guard to ensure that the re-negotiated better deal does not get forgotten as time goes by.

BOUNDARIES AS BASIS FOR MUTUAL UNDERSTANDING

Another reason why boundaries between people are essential is that your boundaries define you; they are part of your personality.

Each person has their own individual tolerance level of how close other people can come, both in a physical and in an emotional sense. Some people will stand very close to you when they are in conversation, and you can feel yourself automatically backing away because it makes you uncomfortable. Some people are very tactile and may touch your arm when they are speaking with you, perhaps because they want to emphasize a point. You may find this intrusive, but another person may like it. As children get older, their comfort level of being cuddled changes. Whereas babies and very young children can be and have to be touched in the process of feeding, changing nappies, bathing and so on, children very soon develop independence as they begin to walk, talk and explore the world around them. With growing self-awareness, they will also develop a very clear sense of who can lift them up and cuddle them and who cannot. Together with their growing body awareness, children also begin to need a sense of privacy where they are allowed to use the toilet on their own as well as bathe themselves without having an adult around.

Apart from these developmental physical boundaries which are set naturally, we all have emotional boundaries, and if these thresholds are overstepped, we get upset. Genetic make-up and personality will determine how much we are affected by emotional stress and how we ultimately deal with it. Two people can be caught in the same situation and react very differently. They may be the same age, the same gender, they may come from a very similar family and schooling background and yet, when the fire alarm goes off in the house, one of them panics and the other one acts calmly. Similarly, when they have been overlooked for promotion, one of them lets it ride, the other one takes it up with the boss.

People are defined by their self-image and by the image they present to the outside world. The amount of control they feel they have over their life is a crucial element in how they think about themselves and others, and the presence of this sense of

8

THE IMPORTANCE OF LOVE

MANKIND IS usually suspected of being primarily selfish, hence the admonition in the Bible to love your neighbour as yourself. This is fair advice, considering that this implies that it is acceptable to love yourself. Your attention is merely drawn to the requirement of a balance between self-love and love of others.

It may be a home truth, but it still needs to be emphasized that you cannot really love anyone else unless you love yourself. When I speak about love in this context, I'm not just referring to that inner warm feeling towards someone else, but also about the courage and willingness to protect the other person, to stand by them in times of trouble and to let them go if that is necessary for their wellbeing. This wider interpretation of 'love' also allows for differences of opinion between people, provided these differences do not lead to behaviour that harms one party. However, the fundamental importance of this particular interpretation of the term 'love' only becomes clear when you apply it to *both yourself and others*. Just as you need to strive to cherish and protect others, so you need to cherish and protect yourself. A man who does not like himself cannot love a partner, he can at most *need* him or her. A woman who does not love herself will not deem herself worthy of protection and will therefore stay with a violent husband, even after repeated beatings.

Turning the other cheek in this context becomes a consent to abuse which demonstrates a sad lack of self-respect, rather than exemplary humility. There is no need to retaliate in kind, but there is a need to remove yourself from the presence of the abusive person. Love cannot be one-directional – if it is applied to others, it also has to be applied to oneself.

TAKING YOURSELF SERIOUSLY

Why is it so hard for some people to respect themselves? What makes them put themselves down when others can see their good points? Why does it make so little difference to their self-esteem if you tell them on a daily basis that they are worthwhile and doing well?

A belief is a formidable emotional force, and once one has become established in your mind, it is difficult to shift or change it. Beliefs about the world and about your own person are formed early on in life. Depending on your personality type, your environment and your circumstances, you begin to build a self-image that reflects how others have treated you. If you spend time with people who don't show any interest in you, you conclude that you are boring and unimportant. If you spend your childhood trying to mediate between incompatible parents, you conclude that the world is an unsafe place and all you can do is try and make it bearable by looking after others. These early lessons are learned quietly, but they are learned solidly. Your beliefs about your place in this world are so enduring because they are usually acquired unwittingly; you don't realize that you hold a particular belief until you are faced with its results. Only when things appear to go wrong frequently do you try and find out why, and only when you get stuck with your own attempts to unravel the knot are you likely to seek professional help. For many people, going for therapy is the first time in their life that they take themselves seriously. Even then their lack of self-esteem shows clearly as they say to the therapist, 'You will probably think this is really silly . . .', or, 'I feel really self-indulgent telling you about myself.'

People who want to gain better self-esteem have to fight two battles, one against their own limiting beliefs and the other one against those around them who have profited from the advantages of living or working with someone who is unconfident. This is when the profiteers try and dissuade the unconfident person from seeking help. It is also the fear that therapy will reveal mistakes that have been made by a client's parents or relations that sometimes makes relatives object to the unconfident person going for therapy, so they press the old button that has worked so well in the past, telling the client-to-be that they are over-sensitive and would do better to pull themselves together rather than waste money on some 'useless' therapy.

People who get stuck in the duty trap are invariably those who don't take themselves seriously. The feeling of being cornered arises from the assumption that you are not allowed to leave this corner, and it is only when you change your attitude about your position that you can improve your situation. Only rarely will this mean having to give up a relationship altogether; but it will always mean re-negotiating the situation, and you can only do this when you insist on your right to be taken seriously. But before you can do that, you have to convince yourself that you have that right.

SELFISHNESS VERSUS SELF-RESPECT

Let me introduce you to a tried and tested concept that has made lots of people unhappy – double standards. Double standards are still alive and kicking, even though their existence is widely denied. There are still industries where women are paid less than men, even though they do the same work; there is still discrimination against coloured people, as there is against other religions and different sexual persuasions. As these double standards are increasingly coming to light these days, legislation has been introduced which seeks to prevent this injustice. However, on an individual level, double standards are still strong and much harder to quash because they are at times subtler and affect mainly a person's emotions which makes it difficult to quantify the damage the person has sustained. The father who steals towels in hotels and laughingly shows off his booty to his family on the journey back home is not just setting a bad example, but is also acting unfairly when he gives his son a sound thrashing for taking something from another child at school. It was just fun when the father did it, but when the child does the same thing it becomes a punishable offence. A mother who prefers her son over her daughter may show this by letting the son get away with bad behaviour, but reprimanding the daughter for the slightest misdemeanour. And even when it is just a matter of your elderly mother clutching her heart every time you make moves to go out, double standards are at play: you are selfish, but she isn't. She is just old and ill and finds it hard to spend an evening on her own.

When you are the person who has drawn the short straw in the game of double standards, you are likely to feel an immense sense of frustration. Even when you address the problem, you are probably going to hear excuses which come in the guise of explanations: 'You are too sensitive!'; 'No wonder nobody likes you – you're always in a bad mood'; 'You are such a difficult person!'; 'You should be a bit more tolerant.' So you stop complaining after a while and start wondering whether maybe you *are* really selfish or difficult.

EXAMPLE
Greg (18) was on the warpath with his father Bernard, a censorious man who could get very unpleasant if Greg did not tow the line. Extremely untidy himself, Bernard became very annoyed if Greg did not keep his room immaculate. At one stage, he even threw all of Greg's belongings out of the

first-floor window into the front garden, just because he did not approve of the state of his room. Bernard would also persistently criticize Greg's driving, while he broke every rule in the book when he took his own car out on the road.

Greg felt deeply frustrated with the situation. 'It feels like I'm allergic to my father. He only has to open his mouth and I want to scream. I just cannot stand his self-righteous way of preaching one thing and doing another. You should see his office; it's like a tip!' Greg attempted to reason with his father in a grown-up manner on several occasions, but Bernard would not have any of it. In the end, Greg felt he just had to move out.

While you are still a child or teenager living at home, there is very little you can do to right these wrongs. You cannot make someone else understand something they don't want to understand. But later in life, when you can stand on your own two feet, you need not take these double standards lying down. The chances are, however, that you have got so used to being treated unfairly that you keep on doing what you have always done – seethe on the inside, but say nothing.

The good news is that you can learn to overcome this impasse (see Part III). Selfishness is *not* the same thing as self-respect. When you find that you are expected to do something which nobody else is prepared to do, you have a right to question or even refuse the demand. Just as you respect other people's needs, so others have to respect yours. No double standards please, and certainly not in your own head!

STOP SMOKE-SCREENING YOUR FEELINGS

One of the main requirements for keeping a reasonable balance between other people's needs and your own is honesty. This means deleting the phrase 'I should' from your mental repertoire, especially when it comes to your own feelings. Every time you think 'I should', you are diffusing and thereby confusing a perfectly valid feeling, making it into an inner conflict area which then gets hard to disentangle. When you are looking after young children and you get to a point where you feel constantly irritated with them, there is no point in giving yourself a hard time because you 'should' feel more affectionate and be more patient. By blaming yourself, you are only adding an extra problem to the existing one; you don't just feel irritated, but guilty as well. Now you are truly stuck; instead of dealing with the original feeling of irritation, you are wasting your time by agonizing over the fact that it is there at all.

The nice thing about feelings is that they are spontaneous. They come straight from the gut level and are pure subconscious material which has nothing to do with logic. This is why thinking 'I should' makes no sense. You feel as you do for a reason. This is not to say that you should not work on making yourself feel better; on the contrary. But this remedial self-developmental work can only succeed if you allow yourself to look at and acknowledge the original feeling, which in our example is the irritation. You can then work your way backwards to find the *reason* for your irritation, which may not necessarily be the children. As you ask yourself who or what is getting on your nerves, you may find that you have worries about money or that there is a problem with your partner or with a colleague at work. Once you understand what has caused your irritation in the first place, you can proceed to take some positive action to resolve it. And even if it is your children who are causing your aggravation, it is still more constructive to try and fathom out a way in which you can tackle the situation than to waste your emotional energy on feeling guilty about being a bad parent. Guilt should only ever be a short-term reminder that a matter needs attending to; as a punishment, guilt is useless because it does not lead to valid solutions.

There is no need to feel bad about 'bad' feelings, but it is important to make an effort to get to the bottom of what is niggling you. You owe it to yourself to investigate if unpleasant emotions arise whenever you find yourself in a particular situation. In this way, you avoid dumping your discontent onto others which only creates more bad feelings and doesn't solve anything. If someone else upsets you by their actions, you have to calm down first and decide what *you* want before you can put your alternatives to the other person.

Having unpleasant feelings like anger, impatience, resentment or jealousy does not make you into a bad person. You do, however, have a responsibility towards yourself and others to ensure that you own up to those feelings, because only then do you give yourself a chance of resolving them. Feelings are there for a reason; that reason lies either in your present circumstances or in your past. Sometimes your present situation can *remind* you of something that has happened in the past, and that makes you react in a similar way to how you did when the original event occurred. In this case, you may need some outside help to overcome your habitual emotional reactions, but there is also a lot you can do by yourself to overcome past trauma.

Part III

CLIMBING OUT OF THE TRAP

9

LEARNING TO UNDERSTAND
YOURSELF

CONSIDERING YOU have spent every single day of your life with yourself, it seems strange to assume that you may not really understand what you are all about. Yet many people genuinely do not know or do not want to admit to themselves what they need in life to be happy. This can happen because others have paid little or no attention to their needs or because the expression of their needs was negatively received in the past. People who find themselves trapped in a life where satisfying other people's demands is the main focus have forgotten who they are, and are often completely unaware that they have lost themselves in the process. Women in particular are prone to getting caught up in caring for others, partly through their biological predisposition, and partly through the expectations of a culture and society that allocate nurturing and supportive activities to women. But men who have a greater percentage of feminine traits in their emotional make-up are just as much at risk.

Once you have lost track of yourself, you have to virtually learn how to regain access to your own person, your wishes and needs. This may appear self-indulgent at first, but it is a fundamental step towards getting out of the duty trap. It may well be more comfortable to continue living with the feelings of inadequacy and guilt than to strive for greater happiness and taking the associated risks of being deemed a heartless person. For many it boils down to a choice of either putting themselves down for not trying harder to do their duties without resentment, or being put down by others for being cruel and unfeeling as they are beginning to take into account their own needs. Many find it is safer to live with the emotional agony they inflict on themselves than with the disapproval inflicted by others.

But disapproval by others is not an inevitable consequence; it *may* happen, but does not have to. You may find that you are getting support from the most unexpected quarter. Much will also depend on how you present your case, and how firmly you stand by what you have said. Rather than ruining relationships, an open word about a problem, together with a negotiated concept of how to resolve the difficulty, can enhance a relationship and make it closer.

WHOSE EXPECTATIONS ARE RUNNING YOUR LIFE?

In order to assess where you stand at the moment, you may find it useful to answer the following questions.

- Do you tend to criticize yourself a lot?
- Do you worry a lot?
- Do you spend a lot of time going over mistakes you have made in the past?
- Do you find it hard to forgive yourself when you have made a mistake?
- Do you always find excuses for other people when they hurt you?
- Do you spend a lot of time trying to understand others so you can make sense of why they are as they are?
- Are your days spent doing things for others?
- Do people frequently come to you for help and support?
- Do the same people criticize you a lot and point out your shortcomings?

- Do you feel a failure?
- Do you expect a lot of yourself, but nothing from others?
- Do you feel treated badly by people around you?
- Do you dislike protesting when you are treated badly?
- When there is a conflict of interests, do you usually lose out?

The more 'yes' answers you have, the lower your confidence and self-esteem, and the more likely it is that you have already fallen into the duty trap. When you forgive others easily and find explanations for their mistakes or their unpleasant behaviour, you are saying that they are right and they have good reasons to be rude, angry or upset with you. At the same time, you disqualify your own feelings as unimportant and blame yourself for anything unpleasant that is said or done to you. It is not just that other people put you down; you pile on the blame by continuing the self-criticism in your own head. This means that your self-assessment is determined by what others say about you, and because you seem unable to meet their expectations, you end up feeling bad about yourself. At the same time, you have no real expectations of others. You may feel a twinge of annoyance at their inconsiderate behaviour and unreasonable demands, but because you are sure that *your inefficiency is the cause of their rudeness* you remain trapped.

Switching Sides Exercise

- For a moment, put yourself into the shoes of someone who is presently giving you a hard time, either by constantly making demands on you or by criticizing you a lot.
- Recall how this person expresses their demands and in which way they criticize you.
- Imagine that you are now acting in this same way towards another person, using the same language. How does this make you feel?

The chances are that you feel quite uncomfortable. Ask yourself why. Is it because the way you make a demand is expressed in a rude manner? Or because you feel the demand is inconsiderate? Or because you feel you would hurt the other person's feelings by criticizing them in this way? Take the time to pinpoint what it is that would bother you if you were asked to speak to someone else as you are being spoken to. As you establish what behaviour you expect of yourself, you are getting closer to discovering what you can expect of others.

- Do you expect yourself to be polite to others?
- Do you expect yourself to be considerate towards others?

If you do, then you have a right to expect the same treatment in return. No double standards please!

It is permissible and sometimes necessary to criticize and to make demands, but it needs to be done in a way that leaves the other person's dignity intact.

WHY ARE YOU STUCK?

After you have sat in the duty trap for some time, you become used to the misery of your situation. After a while, it is easy to forget that there is any other way to live except being there for others all the time, supporting, understanding and being taken for granted.

- Can you imagine that your situation could change for the better in the foreseeable future?

If you can't, either your situation is exceptionally dire or you have lost touch with the possibilities of change. When you have become used to stress and pressure, your mind begins to adapt to it and the stress fails to register consciously. It is at this point that physical or emotional symptoms begin to appear. Anxiety, depression, headaches, tics, lack of concentration and poor memory are frequently signs that something is weighing you down, especially when these symptoms are unusual for you.

- Is there anything you could do to change your situation for the better?

Think *very carefully* about this question. Is there really nothing you could do to improve matters? If you cannot come up with an answer to this question, change it slightly and ask yourself the following:

- Is there anything *a confident person* could do to change a situation like yours for the better?

Would they perhaps address the problem more clearly with the person concerned? Would they be clearer about what they want? Would they refuse to be fobbed off by excuses or dismissive comments? Would they insist on negotiating a better deal for themselves? Would they stand by what they said and hold the other person to what they had promised to change? In other words, are there in fact solutions to your problem, only you feel *you* can't implement them because you are not confident enough?

Check through the following list of reasons which explain why the majority of people get stuck.

- *Self-inflicted burden*
Everyone else urges you to stop doing an unpleasant task but you feel you have to do it because no one else wants to.
- *Disorganization*
You have too much on because you have not planned how to run your life, or if you have, you don't stick to your plan. You waste a lot of time on insignificant details and then don't get the essentials done.
- *Guilty conscience*
You need to appease your conscience over a past mistake and turn the self-punishment into a life sentence for yourself.

• *Lack of conviction*
You are not quite sure whether you are right to feel reluctant to do a particular task. Uncertainty and self-doubt stop you from taking positive action.

• *Sweeping your feelings under the carpet*
You simply pretend that there is no problem because there should not be a problem. This works well until the internal pressure is released as a physical or mental symptom.

• *Fear of hurting someone else's feelings*
You cannot stand your situation any more, but if you abdicated your duty, you are afraid that someone else would feel hurt, so you decide that it is better that you should get hurt instead.

• *Stubbornness*
You could make your situation better, but you don't see why it is always you who has to make the first step to sort out a problem.

• *Damned if you do, damned if you don't*
The other person is genuinely in need of help and there is really no one else to do the job except you, but it is difficult for you to help because you are under pressure yourself.

With all these reasons, there is a component of anxiety and lack of confidence which is behind those feelings of being unable to change an untenable situation.

Underlying these reasons that block your progress are certain unhelpful attitudes. Do you recognize any of these?

• Assuming that something terrible will happen if you act more assertively.
• Wanting to be loved and approved of by everyone around you, and unless they do, you have to be unhappy.
• Wanting to appear to be always in control, and to have all the answers.
• Not wanting to admit that you have a problem with a particular issue.
• Considering yourself to be a victim who is unable to defend her or himself.

- Assuming that you must always do everything for everybody all the time.
- Assuming that everyone else is more important than you are.

You will find ways of dealing with those limiting feelings in the next few chapters.

WHAT DO YOU NEED TO MAKE YOU HAPPIER?

You are doing your duty, you are complying with what is expected of you, and you feel unhappy. You may be doing work in the office which is really someone else's responsibility; you spend time with your husband's ageing mother because your husband is too busy; you mediate between your grown-up sisters because they are constantly rowing and it upsets your parents. You are exhausted, you have had enough, but somehow you cannot stop yourself from continuing to do what you don't want to do any longer.

If asked for a solution, many people want to wish the whole situation away. 'If they hadn't had this department reorganization, I wouldn't have to do two people's jobs'; 'If John made a bit more of an effort with his mother, I wouldn't have to spend a whole day entertaining her while he goes off with his father having a good time'; 'If only my sisters stopped fighting, I could have some peace and quiet.' Well, the department *did* get reorganized, your husband is not particularly fond of his cantankerous mother and your sisters *don't* get on, and there is nothing you can do about it. You cannot change other people's feelings.

What you *can* do something about is your own attitude, together with the way you are dealing with the situation. This is where your responsibility towards yourself comes into play (see p.50). So go back over your situation and analyse what you can do that would make matters easier. Stick with the facts as they are now rather than how they once were before the problem arose.

Heavy workload

- Is the situation temporary or is there no end in sight? Do you need to look for another job?
- Can anyone else help and, if so, have you talked to that person?
- Are you prioritizing adequately, or do you get bogged down with detail? What needs to change is the heaviness of the workload before you collapse. It may seem the wrong time, but it is *now* that you need to stop and consider whether relief is available, or if looking for another job is the only alternative.

Problems in the family

- Is your husband aware of your discontent? Have you *actually asked him* to help you by staying around more when his parents come visiting?
- Are you letting his mother run the way the afternoon goes?
- Do you passively listen to hours of gossip or criticism without changing the subject or asking her to speak about something more pleasant?
- Have you negotiated for the visits to be less frequent?

In this example, several things will probably have to change for you to be happier. Not only do you need to ask your husband for support, but you would also need to find a way of bringing it to his mother's attention that you do not enjoy being criticized all afternoon. This does not necessarily have to be done harshly; you can do it in a joking way.

Problems between siblings

- Is it necessary for you to take on board your parents' upset? Are you personally affected by the sisters' rowing?
- If the rows don't bother you, would it be better for your parents to deal with your sisters directly?
- Has your mediation really made a difference to the frequency or severity of your sisters' rows? If not, what is the point of continuing to mediate?

What needs to change here is your understanding of your role in the family. You may have played mediator and appeaser for many years, but this does not mean you cannot change the part you play in the family constellation. As long as people are unwilling to negotiate, you are wasting your efforts on something that is doomed to fail. It is honourable to want to spare your parents from upset, but you need to recognize your limits in achieving this.

YOU CANNOT SAVE OTHERS

There are certain relationship constellations where one person appears to be particularly vulnerable, while the other person has taken it upon themselves to alleviate their partner's misery.

EXAMPLE
Sam (45) desperately wants to settle down and puts pressure on his partner Vivian to get married so they can have children before it is too late. He is insecure, jealous and possessive. Vivian is not happy in the relationship and wants out, but every time she announces that she has decided to leave him, he breaks down in tears, assures her that they can make it work and that she is all he has. His previous relationships broke up because of his insecurities,

and he now believes that this is his last chance of happiness. Vivian is torn between wanting to go and feeling guilty for inflicting all this unhappiness on Sam, when she knows she could make him feel so much better if only she agreed to marry him.

Unfortunately, this is a false assumption. As long as Sam stays insecure and unconfident, nobody will make him happy in the long run. Even though Vivian has never given him the slightest reason to doubt her trustworthiness, he rings her several times each day to check up on her, picks her up from evening classes and makes such a fuss when she wants to go out for a drink with colleagues after work that she has abandoned the idea of occasionally going out by herself altogether.

No matter how much she reassures him and tries to convince him of her integrity, he cannot ultimately believe her, and this will not change, even if she agrees to marry him. His happiness does not depend on her staying with him but on him sorting out his insecurities and low self-esteem. He tells her that she can save him, because that is what he wants to believe. The truth is that she can never be his saviour; only he can save himself by acting on the realization that he has an emotional problem.

Many people who find themselves sitting in the duty trap feel a strong responsibility for making their problematic partner's life happier. Insecure themselves, these saviour personalities vacillate between the unbearable suppression of their own needs and wanting to make everything all right for the other person. It is only when they understand that this sacrifice is in vain that they can extricate themselves. If they don't manage to do so, there are two people drowning rather than one. As long as there is someone there to buoy them up, the problem partner will never make the effort to learn how to swim.

10

Taking Positive Action To Increase Confidence

THE GREATEST stumbling block for people who want to increase their confidence and self-respect is that they don't think it is something they really deserve, and that is why they assume it is wrong to want it in the first place. 'Who am I to want to focus all that attention on myself? I can never justify this when there are so many people in the world who are worse off than me.' This is a neat and apparently honourable way of outmanoeuvering your needs, but it is about as useful as shooting yourself in the foot. Your needs won't go away just because you think you shouldn't have them.

A lack of self-worth can usually be traced back to one of two sources: either someone has treated you as if you were of no importance, or you have done something in the past which has shattered your self-respect. Consequently, you built up a negative self-image which dominates your thoughts and colours everything you do, and therefore you cannot but come to the conclusion that any attempts at liking yourself better would only be a complete waste of time.

Whenever you catch yourself entering that downward spiral, ask yourself whether you would be just as dismissive if a close friend wanted to work on feeling better about herself. Would you really turn around and tell her she didn't deserve it? No double standards please!

UNDERSTANDING YOUR HISTORY

Our self-image and the degree to which we experience self-respect depends entirely on the set of beliefs we hold. What most people don't realize is that beliefs are acquired through experience. You virtually *learn* to believe certain things about yourself and others through what is happening to you during your lifetime. Your experiences, and especially those during your younger years, can result in either productive or limiting beliefs. Once a belief is firmly established, it acts as a filter on the outside world. Anything that doesn't fit through your belief-filter will simply not register with you.

EXAMPLE
Robert (32) has learned early on in life that his opinion doesn't count. Ever since then, he expects other people to treat him with disrespect, and because this belief makes him feel uncomfortable, he has worked very hard to attain a professional position in life where others *have* to take him seriously because he is the boss. But in spite of his visible success, he still holds the same old beliefs he acquired as a child. This means that whenever anybody is late for an appointment with him, Robert immediately 'knows' that this person is doing it to show Robert how unimportant he is. Whenever people listen attentively to a talk he is giving, Robert 'knows' that they are only pretending to be interested; they don't really respect Robert's expertise. Once they are out of the door, Robert expects them to dismiss what he said as irrelevant.

Robert's belief-filter says that others don't respect him. If he gets a message from others that says something positive about him, for example if someone compliments him on a piece of work, this information runs contrary to his belief, so he inwardly rejects the compliment as insincere or manipulative.

However, when something untoward happens, for example if he cannot get hold of someone on the phone or if someone is rude to him, these messages get straight through to him, *confirming* that nobody respects him; in other words, any negative information that comes from the outside world is eagerly added as 'evidence' that his belief is quite correct. In this way, the negative belief is consistently reinforced because anything that could serve to contradict it is simply never allowed through.

This mechanism of reinforcing a destructive belief is particularly apparent in anorexia sufferers. Their belief that they are fat is so strong that any other information which contradicts this is automatically dismissed. Whether they are told that they look like a skeleton or whether they are shown that they are dangerously underweight, they continue to refuse food. They 'know' that they look better when they are as thin as possible. In extreme cases, beliefs can be so strong that they can kill you or someone else, as is the case with fervent racism or nationalism.

In order to understand which limiting beliefs are running your life, you have to take a look at what has happened to you in the past. If you feel you lack self-esteem, ask yourself the following questions.

Key questions
- **When** did you learn to believe that you are unimportant?
- **Who** taught you to believe that your person or your needs are immaterial?
- **Which event** taught you to believe that you are worthless?

You might find it useful to try to remember if you have always lacked confidence. Even though you have become used to a low level of self-respect, this may not have always been so. Has there been a time when you were happier about yourself? Pinpointing the approximate period where the change occurred can help answer the next two questions, namely which person, or what event, subdued your sense of self-worth.

EXAMPLE
Christina (28) was struggling with low self-esteem, and as a consequence, she was stressed, short-tempered and felt out of control. She was very self-critical and felt inadequate as a mother to her two-year-old daughter because she felt constantly torn between doing household chores, running errands and trying to give attention to her little girl. Christina's memories centred around a period of time between the ages of eight and ten where she had stolen things from other children, and she felt so bad about her childhood misdemeanours that it had coloured her self-image ever since.

But even though Christina thought that her problems began around the time when she started stealing, closer inspection revealed that it had started before then. With children, stealing is usually a comfort activity that tries to make up for something else that is missing, and in Christina's case it turned out to be parental affection. The loveless atmosphere at home had made her feel unhappy and unwanted, and taking nice things from other children was an attempt at redressing the balance. Once Christina understood the *context* in which her stealing had occurred, she could see it in proportion. She became much more relaxed generally and began to fully enjoy spending time with her daughter.

In trying to answer any of the three key questions, it pays to be as honest as possible. There is no need to protect anyone and there is no point in kidding yourself. It is not disloyal to admit it if one or both of your parents were unkind. This is not about apportioning blame; this is about clarifying what led you to adopt limiting beliefs about yourself. Equally, if a particular past event upset you greatly at the time, don't dismiss it out of hand as a possible cause for your lack of self-esteem just because it happened a long time ago or because you now assume that you over-reacted at the time.

If you find it difficult to answer any of the three key questions, make a list of all the memories you have of distressing events in your life. Here are a few situations which tend to cause anxiety and stress.

- Being ignored or neglected as a child.
- Having other siblings preferred over you because they are better-looking, more intelligent, more sporty, and so on.
- Being frequently criticized and reprimanded.
- Witnessing frequent rows between parents.
- Witnessing or experiencing violence or abuse in the family.
- Being bullied at home by other siblings, at school by other pupils or at work by colleagues.
- Moving frequently and not being able to settle down and make long-term friends.
- Failing frequently, either academically, at work or in relationships.
- The death of a close family member, a close friend or a much-loved pet.
- A new baby in the family.
- Someone close to you or yourself suffering a serious illness.
- A considerable deterioration in your living conditions.

These are only a few situations which can cause you to lose your confidence, and they are just meant to jog your memory. Once you have made your own list, continue as follows.

Memory Exercise
- With your eyes closed, let each of the listed memories pass briefly through your mind.

- Notice your gut reaction to each one and select that memory which evokes the strongest feelings in you.
- Write down this memory in as much detail as you can.
  (In the unlikely event that you find yourself getting unduly upset while going over a memory, you should stop this exercise immediately and consider seeking professional help. At the end of the book, you will find addresses of organizations which can help.)

Even if you were able to answer only one of the three key questions, it still makes sense to establish your list of upsetting life events for the next exercise.

Self-appreciation Exercise
- Despite past upsets, you are still here to tell the tale. Think about which inner qualities have helped you come through, maybe a bit worse for wear, but still alive and kicking.
- Write down your strong qualities. Make several copies of this list and keep one by your bedside, one in your handbag or briefcase, stick one on the mirror in the bathroom and one on the inside of your front door.
- Whenever you find yourself spiralling down into negative thoughts about yourself, get into the habit of adding, 'Be that as it may, but it is also true to say that I have some good qualities!' and recite them to yourself.

Always remember that whatever wrong you may have done you can make up for it, and you can overcome any trauma you have experienced; there is no need to stay stuck in the past. Rescue is possible, solutions can be found and happiness can become a reality.

DILEMMAS – TAKING A LONG-TERM VIEW

Dilemmas can present themselves in many ways. You may have small children who you have to leave with your parents in the daytime because you need the income your job generates to keep the family finances afloat. You want to spend more time with your children, and you also feel guilty for using your parents as babysitters. On top of all that there is the added difficulty that you don't agree with your father's attitude to certain issues concerning your children, but there is no way you could financially afford leaving the children with a childminder. You feel unable to change your situation.

Someone else may find that they are working very hard in their job without getting acknowledgement for their efforts. There are successfully completed projects that prove their competence, and yet no promotion is on the horizon. The job market looks dire, and our friend feels that it will be difficult to find employment in his specialized field anyway. He feels truly stuck in his situation.

When you are on the horns of a dilemma, it can feel as if you are standing against the wall in a room that you suspect has alarms everywhere. You expect that as soon as you move away from the wall, something is going to go off which will make you jump out of your skin with fright, so that all you would want to do is to get back to your old position against the wall where you may feel stuck, angry and frustrated, but at least you don't have to be afraid. Maybe your fear of moving away from the wall is based on experience – when you tried before, you set off an almighty racket. Maybe someone has impressed on you that it would be silly or presumptuous to want to move away from your present position. Or maybe the rest of the room and the open door at the other end did not look enticing enough to warrant the emotional upheaval of getting away from the wall.

While you are still stuck you might as well make use of your time in a constructive way by assessing your prospects. The reason why it makes sense to think about the future and your long-term aims in life is because you will need a goal to work towards, otherwise there is very little incentive to move away from the wall. Also, if you allow your frustration to build up to unmanageable proportions, you will eventually implode or explode. Pent-up emotions eventually have to be discharged. Once you have reached breaking point, they are released either against yourself which means you become exhausted or depressed, or they are released against the outside world via angry outbursts or moodiness. For our example of the mother with young children, this could mean that ultimately the relationship with her husband could become strained, or she might find herself to be short or irritable with the children which then makes her feel even more useless as a mother.

In order to assess your present problematic situation, take a moment to consider the following questions.

Key Questions

- How frustrated and/or exhausted do you feel at the moment? Give yourself a score on a scale from 1 to 10, with 1 being only mildly frustrated and 10 being close to a nervous breakdown.
- Is your present situation temporary or long term?
- If you call your present situation temporary, is that because there are objective facts that indicate that you will soon be over the worst, or do you just *hope* that it is temporary?
- If your situation is long term, is there an end in sight? If so, when? Again, ask yourself whether your assessment is based on facts or on hopes.

The higher your score on the frustration/exhaustion scale, the more urgently you need to look at the time scale of your problem. As your energy levels deplete, it becomes more difficult to make rational assessments because your emotions take over and cloud your vision while you just go on doing what you feel you have to do like a (bad-tempered) robot. Ideally, you deal with your dilemma right at the start when it has only just turned out that you have a problem. While you are still feeling fresh and rational, you are most likely to come up with a workable solution. However, once a short-term dilemma is allowed to develop into a long-term problem, your chances that you come out unscathed diminish, and the changes required to set right the situation become more difficult to implement, with a high price to pay for everyone involved.

EXAMPLE

Helen (25) had been living with Tom for six years. They wanted children but decided not to marry, and they now had two little boys, aged two and three.

Helen's relationship with Tom had never really worked. From the beginning, Tom had been unpredictable and unreliable, and Helen had thought of leaving him many times, but each time she made an attempt to go, he begged and pleaded with her and she ended up staying. Helen had hoped that things would change once the boys were there because Tom had always been very keen on children. Instead, Tom became even worse. They were rowing more and more frequently because he often stayed out until late during the week, and on weekends he would sometimes disappear altogether, leaving Helen and the children on their own.

Helen realized that she needed to become more independent so she could eventually leave Tom, and she decided to go to an evening class to learn book-keeping. Tom, however, stayed his old unreliable self and often did not keep to his promise to be home in time for Helen to go off to her class, so she missed too many lessons and finally had to give up. What she really wanted to do was walk away from everything, but she loved her children and told herself that at least Tom was a good provider and she didn't want the boys to grow up without a father. Over the following year, she developed a severe anxiety disorder.

Helen's case history illustrates clearly how a problem can get out of hand if you don't tackle it while it is still manageable. It is not that Tom became unreliable overnight; he had always been like that. Helen wanted to leave him several times, even before the children were there. If at that time she had been asked to answer the Key Questions (p. 76), she would have had to say that she was extremely frustrated and that there was no end in sight to Tom's irresponsible behaviour. Her hopes that he might change for the better were based not on facts but merely on his promises that he would be home more often if only they had children.

Every time Helen let herself be persuaded against her better judgement, she dug herself deeper into a hole, losing more and more self-esteem and confidence, until she was stuck with two small children, no job qualifications and no prospects of becoming independent financially.

When you answer the Key Questions, you are helping yourself become more aware of where you stand with your present situation. This is a good starting point, but it is not enough. You now need to think about where you wanted to go in life *before* you got stuck.

Future Projection Exercise 1
- As best you can, set aside your present situation. Imagine that you are putting all your problems onto a shelf in your mind. As you do so, you are not denying that these problems exist, you are merely getting them out of your mental line of vision. Do this with your eyes closed.
- Now indulge in a little daydream. Where do you want to go in life? What have you always wanted to achieve? What are your very own personal aims in life? Where would you like to be in five years' time? You will know that you have a good aim when you get a positive 'gut-reaction' while thinking about your aim: warmth in the stomach area, deeper breathing or a little surge of positive emotions.

Future Projection Exercise 2
- Now take your present dilemma off that imaginary shelf. Does your current situation allow you to achieve your aim

in the foreseeable future? If not, go on to the next step of this exercise.
- Imagine what your life will be like in five years' time if your dilemma is allowed to exist unchecked. What is your vision of the future? If it looks bleak if your present situation were to continue, it is time for change *now*!

Remember that respect has to cut both ways. You have to respect your children's needs, your partner's needs and your employer's needs, but you *also* have to respect your own. In Helen's case, there is a clear imbalance between her own needs and those of her children. Also, her declaration that the children should not be deprived of their father does not hold water; Tom was never there anyway, so they would not be losing any quality time with him were Helen to leave Tom.

In the end, Helen decided to persevere with her plans of learning about book-keeping. She borrowed some money from a friend and invested in a correspondence course which she studied in the evenings. Her former evening class teacher knew about Helen's situation and agreed to help her if she got stuck with the course material.

Helen was now set to go. She enjoyed filling her evenings with studying, and it actually suited her that Tom came home late. She finished the course and was able to get a part-time job with a small company. She also made enquiries about her legal situation if she were to separate from Tom and found that he would have to provide for the children. She is currently discussing the issue with Tom.

REMOVING STUMBLING BLOCKS

As you have seen in Helen's case history, the hardest bit was to get over the feeling of being stuck and to persevere when initial attempts of freeing yourself do not work out straight away. Climbing out of the duty trap can be hard work, and that is why it is vital to have an aim (see Exercise 1 on p.78) in life for yourself so you can stay focused even when you have the occasional setback.

First of all, check whether you are serious about wanting to improve your present situation.

Key Questions
- Do you derive any *advantages* from remaining stuck?
- Can you meet the other person halfway, or are you stuck in an all-or-nothing attitude?
- What have you done lately to improve your situation?
- How much time do you spend thinking about your problems? How much time do you spend trying to find solutions? How much time do you spend imagining how other people will not let you implement those solutions? How much time do you spend imagining that you are not competent enough to make your solutions work for you?

If you gain something positive for yourself by remaining stuck, you are unlikely to make a determined effort to resolve the problematic situation. If you get attention, or if you exert some form of revenge on someone else by keeping the dilemma as it is, you might suffer, but the pay-off you are getting outweighs the disadvantages. This in turn weakens your resolve to sort matters out.

Most people spend an inordinate amount of time thinking about the problem rather than the solution. Their mind spirals to disaster level as soon as an idea for a solution presents itself, and they systematically set about destroying the idea with negative thinking. And sure enough, the belief that it won't work becomes true – because you cannot believe it can be done, you don't even attempt it, and therefore the idea is never translated into reality. Most ideas die of self-sabotage.

EXAMPLE
Tony (42) had been going out with Marcella for five years, and he adored her. He wanted to get married,

but Marcella put it off; she couldn't make up her mind to go ahead. They had met after Marcella had split up with her previous boyfriend Richard, and Tony reckoned that Marcella needed a bit more time. He knew that Marcella was still in touch with Richard, and that on one occasion, Marcella had even slept with Richard while she was already living with Tony, but she assured Tony that it didn't mean anything and that she only loved him. However, Marcella carried on seeing Richard, and Tony became increasingly distressed. He didn't want to lose Marcella because she was his closest friend and they had spent many happy years together. Marcella assured him that she loved him, but admitted that she needed Richard as well. She told Tony that if he really loved her, he would accept that she wanted to keep seeing Richard. Tony felt that he had to agree to this arrangement. For one thing, he *did* love Marcella, and he also didn't want to be seen as narrow-minded. Tony felt trapped, but he was afraid to vent his anger and disappointment in case it gave Marcella an excuse to leave him altogether. He started drinking, his work suffered and he felt close to a nervous breakdown.

Tony was hanging on to memories of the good old days. Marcella and he had been very happy together, and had been on wonderful holidays. Tony felt he had supported Marcella, encouraged her in her career, been understanding about her need to keep in touch with her ex-boyfriend and had even forgiven her for ending up in bed with Richard. And now she had practically moved out.

Tony's greatest stumbling block is probably his own naivety concerning Marcella's relationship with Richard. Tony did not see what he did not want to see, even though the facts were right before him. Marcella had never really got over Richard, and that was why she didn't want to marry Tony.

In order to help Tony see the situation for what it was, I took him through the following exercise.

Screen Exercise 1
- Sit down and close your eyes.
- Think about your current situation. Remember all the details about what is happening in your difficult situation at the moment.
- Imagine that you could put all the events of the last few months onto a screen in your mind. In your mind, see everything that has been happening as an outside observer. Replace your own person on the screen with a very good friend, or maybe with a close relative who you like a lot. See happening to them what is happening to you at the moment.
- Check how you feel about your friend on the screen who is in your place.
- Check how you feel about the other person who is making the demand on your friend.

When Tony watched someone else in his position, his instant reaction was clear – this situation was quite unacceptable, and so were the demands made by the girlfriend on the screen. When I asked Tony what advice he would give to his friend on the screen, Tony's answer was, 'That woman is not good enough for you. Throw her out!'

Try out Exercise 1 for your own situation. It is very important to express your feelings in words, so once you are aware of your feelings towards the individual participants on the screen, continue as follows.

Screen Exercise 2
- As an outside observer, walk onto the screen and express very clearly how you feel about the demanding person's behaviour. Don't be worried about going overboard; it's fine if you want to imagine yourself shouting.
- Now go over to your friend on the screen and encourage him or her. Tell them they don't have to put up with these conditions and demands, tell them they deserve better.

- Come out of the screen again and check how you feel now.

The screen is a place in your mind where it becomes possible to look at your present situation more objectively. By putting someone else into your shoes and watching them from the outside, you can assess better whether you are really over-sensitive or whether someone else is making unreasonable demands on you.

Use the screen to vent your feelings. The screen is not reality; the screen is a place where you can let off steam symbolically. This is helpful because it clarifies how you really feel about your situation once you get a wider perspective. The surer you are of your feelings, the easier it is to make decisions and stand by them later on.

Once you have clarified how you feel about your difficult situation, you will need to get your actions in line with your feelings. For Tony, this meant having to speak to Marcella about how he felt about the situation and what he wanted for the future. By now, Tony was clear that he felt betrayed by Marcella, and even though he still loved her, he was no longer willing to put up with her demand that he should tolerate her affair with Richard. Having done the Future Projection Exercises (p.78), Tony had established that he wanted to get married and have children, and with Marcella unwilling to commit herself, this was unlikely to happen. Hard as it was, he had to confront Marcella with the choice between him and Richard. This could of course mean that Tony might lose Marcella to Richard, but he decided that a painful end to the relationship would ultimately be preferable to the prolonged agony of not knowing where he stood.

When you broach a subject that involves your own and other people's feelings, there are a few ground rules that you should observe.

- The higher the emotional content of the problem, the more important the choice of where you have your conversation.

Neutral territory such as a public place can be a good choice because it forces everyone involved to keep their emotions in check.

- Keep it simple and don't beat about the bush. Identify the issue and stick to it. Repeat what it is you want; don't let yourself be deflected by counter-challenges.
- Before you have your meeting, take out some time to anticipate the other person's reactions and make plans how you will deal with them.
- Be firm, not aggressive. Express your feelings as part of your message but not as all of it.

Tony met Marcella in a restaurant for lunch. He explained that he wanted her to make up her mind because he was no longer willing to tolerate the present situation, and he wanted her to move out. He suggested that they cease contact for three months and that she could then let him know what her decision was. Marcella burst into tears and tried to dissuade Tony from making the break, but also admitted that she could not decide which man she wanted to be with. Tony stayed firm and Marcella moved out. After three months, Marcella was still unable to make a decision, so Tony decided to break it off. After some time on his own, he met someone else and got married to a woman who was sure she wanted him and no one else.

COMING OFF THE GUILT TRIP

Feeling guilty is a particularly potent form of self-torture. You do not need other people to give you a bad time, you can make yourself miserable in a matter of seconds! In order to escape the self-inflicted pressure, you are then driven to try and make up for your perceived short-comings, and this makes you an ideal candidate for the duty trap.

Having a conscience is basically a good thing. As we all have to share this world with other people, we need to have a sense of responsibility, and we also need to show respect for other people's needs. These qualities are usually acquired during childhood and adolescence as part of the socialization process, with parents and teachers providing instruction about what is right and what is wrong. But during this process of becoming a fully fledged member of society things can go wrong. A lot will depend on how sensible a teacher you had when you learned to have a conscience.

Learning to become a responsible adult is an emotional matter. As children, our first and probably natural instinct is to do what *we* want to do and to see to our own needs first. As we get older, we gradually learn that we have to curb our desire for instant self-gratification – we have to wait for things we would rather have straight away, and some things we want we cannot have at all. Sometimes we have to share something with another person when we would rather have it all to ourselves, and we also have to learn to show gratitude and display other social niceties when we deal with others. In this context, it is important for a young person to be taught a balanced view of the importance of your own needs and those of others, and this is where problems can occur. Some parents bring up their children as if they had no needs or feelings, expecting the children to fit in and be grateful for being given food and a roof over their head. Any signs of independent thinking are consequently treated as wilful insubordination which is labelled 'bad', 'difficult' and 'ungrateful'. In this way, a young person learns to associate any stirrings of a personal opinion as bad, and any sense of their self as wrong.

When the declaration of your own needs, however timidly put, is rewarded by punishment of some sort, you learn to feel guilty every time you want something. Initially, your parents impose the guilt on you; later, once you have internalized it, you take over from your parents and become your own accuser every time you dare think about yourself. By now you understand that others are more important than you, and no matter how much you may rebel against this conclusion intellectually, emotionally it has become an inner truth that forces you to neglect yourself and at the same time elevate others to the position of main protagonists.

Now the door is open to endless self-recrimination which begins to happen silently but very powerfully in your own head. Once you are convinced that you are blameworthy, your life begins to revolve around endless thoughts of what you did wrong in the past and the mistakes you might make in the future. Your negative feelings about yourself are usually borne out (or so you think) by one or several past events which seem to prove your conviction that you are no good.

At this stage, you become easy prey for anyone who wants to make unreasonable demands, manipulate or emotionally blackmail you. All they need to do is confirm what you are thinking about yourself anyway – that you need to do anything you can to make up for your deplorable shortcomings.

Of course we also have to consider the possibility that you have indeed done something in the past which was wrong. You may have left someone in the lurch when you could have helped, you may have been irresponsible with someone else's property or money, or you may have seriously jeopardized your own career by committing an offence. Others might have blamed you, but you blame yourself most, and often you do so many years after the actual event. There may be nothing you can do about that past event now – the person you have let down may long be dead, the damage done lasting and irrevocable. The only option you have is to make sure you apologize if the other person is still around, and make sure that you don't ever get yourself into a situation where you hurt someone else (or yourself) in this way. This may mean joining a rehabilitation programme if you are alcohol-dependent, or going for therapy if an emotional problem has caused you to act or react irresponsibly. It is not good enough just to say sorry and then go and do it again. It is your responsibility to do everything in your power to prevent the repetition of a wrong. However, once you can honestly say that you are working on overcoming your problem, you can let go of your guilt. After all, a guilty conscience is only a signal telling you that a particular matter needs your attention. Once you have acknowledged it by taking positive action, the warning bells no longer need to ring in your head.

In other cases, it is not so clear cut whether you were really at fault, even though the other party assures you that you were. When you find yourself in such a situation, use a variation of the screen exercise.

Screen Exercise 3
- Sit down and close your eyes.
- Think about the situation that made the other person blame you. Think the whole event through in as much detail as possible.
- Now put everything that happened onto your inner mental screen and watch what is going on as a detached outside observer. If necessary, include the wider context in which this event occurred.
- Imagine that you are giving a running commentary to a friend on the phone while you are watching the action unfold on the screen.
- Check how you feel about what you see on the screen.

EXAMPLE
Peter and Paul have been friends for many years. Peter lost his job eighteen months ago, and despite considerable efforts to find a new one, he has not been successful. Even though he is not well off himself, Paul has lent Peter money on a few occasions, always pointing out that Peter must pay it back by a certain time, but so far Peter has not made any attempt at repaying anything. Whenever Paul points out that he himself is caught short unless Peter repays at least some of his debt, Peter says, 'There is nothing I can do, I'll repay you later.'

Before Christmas, Peter approaches Paul with the request for more money because he wants to buy presents for his nephews and nieces. Paul refuses on the grounds that he can't afford to give Peter any more. Also, he explains that presents are not a strict necessity and that the nieces and nephews are old enough to understand that Peter can't give them very much this time. Peter is very angry that Paul refuses to help, and Paul starts feeling really guilty. Maybe he should have helped Peter by using his credit card?

You can see that the context is important in this example. Paul had already helped out several times, and Peter has not paid him back even a fraction so far. This background information has to go onto the screen together with the Christmas presents incident to put the latter into perspective.

But even though getting a more objective view of your situation is helpful, it is not always enough to stop the guilt feelings from going round and round in your mind. You can get yourself into a rut with feeling guilty; your mind just gets used to thinking along particular lines so that you habitually fret and worry. Here are two simple ways in which you can interrupt the involuntary repetitive thoughts about past events that are associated with feelings of guilt.

The Forgetful Sinner Exercise
- If you were at fault, apologize and set right what can still be set right and work on improving yourself. Only then continue with the next step.
- Be clear that your feelings of guilt no longer serve a purpose because the matter is in hand now.
- Whenever you catch yourself going over past events, pretend that the memory is beginning to slip your mind ('What was there on my mind just now? I can't remember – it's gone.')

This exercise works because you are beginning to systematically disrupt the memory flow that brings on the feelings of guilt. No memory, no guilt!

The Newsreader Exercise

- If you have been at fault, apologize and make amends where possible. Work on yourself so that you are unlikely to make the same mistake again. Only then continue with the next step.
- Whenever you catch yourself going over old guilt-inducing memories, stop yourself and start mentally reciting what happened in a factual manner, just quickly going over each part of the event in a matter-of-fact way.

The following case history can serve as an example for this exercise.

EXAMPLE

Carmen (52) had been driving to work when a young man ran out from behind a bus and she knocked him over. He lay motionless by the side of the road. Carmen was deeply shocked and felt very guilty, even though eyewitnesses confirmed that she had been driving at a cautious speed and that it was the young man's fault; he had just started rushing to the other side of the road without checking the traffic first. Carmen could not possibly have prevented the accident, and yet she felt extremely guilty about the man who was now in hospital. In order to overcome her feelings of guilt, Carmen recited the following to herself in a matter-of-fact way, 'I drove along cautiously. A young man rushed out from behind a bus without looking, he collided with my car and was knocked to the ground. He is now in hospital.'

This unembellished and unemotional recital of the facts

helped her take control of the random flow of thoughts and emotions so that she was able to look back on the accident with feelings of regret for the young man but with no feelings of guilt.

However, a guilty conscience can at times be tenacious, and when you have been in the habit of feeling guilty for a long time, you may need to add another, more in-depth exercise to combat the constant self-accusations going through your head. But before you read through the next exercise, accept the following theory for the time being.

- You are basically a good person.
- It is permissible for a good person to make mistakes. Mistakes do not automatically make you into a bad person.

Contact Your Conscience Exercise

- If you have genuinely done someone wrong, apologize and do everything in your power to prevent the same lapse from occurring again.
- Sit down and close your eyes.
  Establish what your conscience is telling you about yourself to make you feel guilty; what are the guilty thoughts that are going through your mind? Examples: 'You are just not trying hard enough'; 'You are incompetent/selfish/unfeeling/a loser'; 'You are too sensitive'; 'You should have tackled the situation differently'; 'You shouldn't have said what you said.'
- Imagine you could take your conscience out and put it in front of you and make it into a person. Notice what your personified conscience looks like. Does it remind you of someone you know?
- Give your personified conscience a name; let's say your conscience is called 'Fred' if you are a man, and 'Gladys' if you are a woman.
- First of all, thank Fred for working to make you into a better and more competent person by alerting you to any mistakes you are making.

- Now explain to Fred that even though you appreciate his good intention, you are not very happy with the *manner* in which he is trying to help you improve yourself.
- Go on to explain that it is no good if he shouts at you or if he is cynical or disdainful because that only makes you more nervous and insecure and less likely to avoid future mistakes.
- Tell Fred that if he really wants to help you, you want him to:
  a) Lower his voice when he is speaking to you.
  b) Cut out the drama when he is pointing out mistakes or shortcomings to you.
  c) Stop repeating the same thing over and over again.
- In return for him doing this for you, you promise to listen attentively to what he is saying, and you will then make concrete plans to amend your shortcomings.
- See if you can get agreement from Fred on this proposal. Agree to review the situation in a week's time.
- Shake hands on the deal.
- Re-integrate Fred into your mind.

Your conscience is part of your mind, which means it is part of your thoughts and your emotions. Unfortunately our mind comes without a user manual, and we usually don't know what we can do to influence it in a positive way. By using the above technique, you are beginning to take charge of what is going on in your mind. There is no need to let your thoughts run riot. Consider yourself the boss and your conscience your employee. Fred's job is to keep a tab on what you are getting up to in your life; it is not to insult you or put you down. You need Fred, but he needs you too, so you might as well start talking to one another and come to an amicable agreement. As the boss, *you* have to provide the job description and you have to make sure that Fred sticks to it. This means that when you notice repeated self-depreciating thoughts coming up, you will have to get Fred out again and remind him of your agreement. If, however, matters have improved after a week, you should still get in touch with him and thank him for his co-operation. Be polite, even if you are only talking to your own conscience!

EXAMPLE

Edward (32) felt very stressed in his new job. The company had employed him to get one of their retail branches back on its feet. Bad management had resulted in financial losses, and Edward's task was to sort matters out.

After four weeks' work, Edward felt as if he had bitten off more than he could chew. He had found that matters were far worse than he had expected, and his workload was enormous. He went in at eight in the morning and rarely left before eight at night. He even went in on weekends. It didn't really bother him that he had practically no social life in the new job. He was single and wanted to build up a good career before settling down. However, he was concerned about the way he felt ever since he took on the new position. He was overwrought, slept badly or not at all, had lost his appetite and worried every waking moment whether he would be able to sort all the problems out and get the branch going again. His strong sense of duty towards the company weighed on him so heavily that he, even after a 12-hour day, felt guilty leaving the office.

When he did the Contact Your Conscience Exercise, his conscience looked like an older man in army uniform who kept telling Edward that he was going to mess things up if he didn't work day and night. Edward called his conscience 'Anthony' because it reminded him a bit of his father whose name was Anthony and who was very strict. Edward gave Anthony some civilian clothes so he looked a bit more casual and also negotiated a more civilized tone when Anthony had something to say.

He soon started sleeping better and began to feel much more optimistic about his chances of success.

11

LEARNING TO UNDERSTAND HIDDEN AGENDA

WHEN YOU find yourself giving in to unreasonable demands again and again, when you are made to feel so guilty for saying 'no' that you eventually retract your objection, or when it is always you who ends up with unpleasant tasks, you should ask yourself whether others are manipulating you. If you have little confidence and low self-esteem you can become an easy target for people who are prone to take advantage of others.

There are a great many ways in which manipulation can happen, and some of these ways can be so subtle that it is hard to be certain whether you are imagining it, or whether the other person is really trying in an underhand way to get you to do things. A further problem can be that there often seems to be a perfectly logical explanation for why the other person gave you a particular look, why they asked you to do something for them or why they keep complaining about you. You think you know why they are reacting to you like that – it is because *you* didn't get it right, because *you* are not very competent, because *you* cannot read their mind as you should be able to do by now. You feel that the other person has to give you a hard time because of your inadequacy as a human being. So you try harder still to please and appease them, but somehow you can never get it right. You think you know why they are like that, but you don't *really* understand. You cannot see that it is convenient for the other person to keep you down because this guarantees your compliance with all sorts of demands that a more confident person would firmly refuse.

On the other hand, we can also sometimes manipulate ourselves by only seeing what we want to see. We defend indefensible behaviour in others, we purposely overlook obvious misdemeanours and we make excuses for people who are doing a lot of emotional damage to others. We can delude ourselves by mentally re-arranging reality in such a way that it fits in with how we want it to be, but there is a price to be paid for not wanting to admit how things really are. Reality has a way of catching up with you which can be more unpleasant and painful than facing the facts in the first place.

MANIPULATION

The most straightforward way of manipulating another person is by bullying them into doing what you want them to do. You can get people to comply with your wishes by making your demands in an aggressive way ('You either do this or . . .'), threatening unpleasant consequences if they don't do as you tell them, or shouting at them ('Do as you are told!'). These methods rely on the recipient being susceptible to these scare techniques, and many people are, especially when they have been subjected to them from an early age.

EXAMPLE
Elizabeth (36) remembers her father shouting down anyone who dared to contradict him. Even his wife was not safe from his wrath if his orders were not carried out to his satisfaction. Elizabeth's father's outbursts scared her so much that she quickly learned to do as she was told and keep her opinion to herself. Over the years, she developed

a great fear of conflict and she tried to avoid any situations which might lead to a confrontation. At the age of 26, she married a man who was an immense improvement on her father, but by this stage Elizabeth had become afraid to say boo to a goose. She had given up having her own opinion and did what she thought were her duties by her husband and later her children, even though it meant doing things that made her unhappy. She had greatly enjoyed working before the children came along, but she felt that she would neglect her duties as a mother if she went back to work before the youngest child was at least 12 years old. Over the years, she developed an anxiety problem which resulted in her being unable to drive her car.

As a child, there is really nothing you can do against a bullying parent. In Elizabeth's case the only person who could have done something was her mother, but she was too frightened herself. The result was that Elizabeth never learned that it is acceptable to have your own opinion. Peace could only be achieved by total compliance with her father; there was no alternative. However, it is perfectly possible to acquire greater confidence later on in life, and in her eight sessions of analytical hypnotherapy, Elizabeth allowed herself to release all the pent-up feelings about her childhood misery, her anger towards the tyrannical father and her disappointment about her mother who had failed to protect her. At the end of her sessions, Elizabeth had gained in confidence considerably and had started driving her car again.

Scare tactics that you are subjected to in younger years can have far-reaching effects, but you can also encounter them later on in life. Military drills involve shouting, often with the officer in charge standing quite close to a soldier's face while he shouts at him. This is accepted practice in the military, but some industrial bosses and managers also seem to subscribe to this technique. Here are a few pointers about what to do should you be forced to work for someone like that.

- Don't confuse the forceful expression of feelings with bullying. Someone can be letting off steam without doing this to punish or blame you.
- If your superior is blaming you in an aggressive way, you have the right to either wordlessly leave the room or to tell him or her that you will come back when he/she has calmed down, and then leave the room. You are not obliged to listen to a torrent of accusations which does not allow for a dialogue.
- If you are being threatened with consequences unless you comply with a request, you have several options. Depending on how seriously you take the threat, you can continue to press the issue and emphasize that you consider the matter as very important, or you can take the issue to a higher authority. If you feel very sure of yourself and your position, you can also call your boss's bluff.

EXAMPLE
John (39) had been working for his new boss for four weeks when he decided he had to have a word. Even though John had been in his job for three years, his new boss insisted on checking up on everything he did. He would even go through the paperwork on John's desk when he wasn't there. The new boss was a nervous man who had a short fuse when someone didn't appear to understand what he was telling him. John was put out by his boss's manner and felt very annoyed at being monitored so closely all the time. He made an appointment to see his boss and explained calmly that he was not happy with being supervised in this way. Before he could finish what he had to say, his boss started yelling that if he didn't like it he could leave. He, the boss, would fire him for insubordination! John did not budge. He confirmed that he knew his boss had the power to fire him, but that he still didn't like his boss rifling through his paperwork when John was not at his desk. Acknowledging the boss's greater power stopped

the boss in his tracks and he calmed down. A reasonable conversation followed where both parties agreed to a new arrangement. It turned out that the boss had been anxious about not being fully informed, so John agreed to meet up with him for 10 minutes every morning to report what had been going on the previous day and briefly discuss what projects he would deal with on that day.

Another form of manipulation is more subtle than the openly aggressive threat, but just as annoying. You don't want to do something, but you are told that it is in your best interest ('It is for your own good!'). You are asked to trust someone else's judgement and hand over responsibility about decisions that concern you. This may be appropriate between a parent and a child, but it is not acceptable between adults. A mother who intercepts phone calls by her adult daughter's lover has no right to do so, even if the lover is a married man. It is an excuse to say that it is her duty to protect her daughter from unhappiness; the mother is interfering.

- Every adult has to take responsibility for their own actions, for their ensuing feelings and for any consequences.
- Before you act or decide on important issues, get your facts straight. If someone else has relevant facts to add, take them into consideration but check them, because in the end it is still only you who is responsible for your final decision.

If someone tries to prevent you from doing what you feel is necessary or right, do not be sidetracked. Thank them for their concern, but tell them that you are an adult and don't need looking after any more.

A variation of this type of manipulation is when you ask for something and the other person listens attentively and agrees with you, but then later on procrastinates and does not do what they said they would. This is a much used method in the legal world and also employed by many companies. They promise they will send you something today ('The cheque is in the post'), and after two weeks you have still not received the item. Agreeing initially is a good way of getting someone off your back for a while. As soon as you say yes to their request, the other party feels relieved and stops making demands.

Manipulative people also sometimes try and stop someone from challenging them by distracting from the real issue, either by ridiculing or counter-challenging the person who confronts them.

EXAMPLE
Ever since her mother died, Erica (36) had had her father come to stay with her and her family every Sunday. The father is and always has been a difficult man. Erica's children try and avoid him because he has nothing but criticism for their behaviour, their clothes and their opinions. Erica does not like her father criticizing her children continuously; it spoils the day for everyone. But whenever she tells her father that she wants him to stop lecturing the children, she gets answers like 'I wouldn't have to tell them off if you were doing a better job as a mother' or 'What are *you* getting upset about? I'm not speaking to you, I'm talking to *them*!'

Erica's father is not responding to her request to stop criticizing the children. Instead, he is making out that it is Erica's incompetence as a mother that forces him to intervene. He also suggests that Erica is over-reacting and that he as the grandfather should have the last word in any matters concerning the children. By asking his daughter to stay out of the conversation, he implies that he is the only responsible adult in the room, and thereby pushes his daughter back into the child role.

What do you do with someone like Erica's father? First of all it is important to check the facts.

- Is his criticism of the children justified? If so, which parts of the criticism are warranted? Clothes and opinions should be up to the children; bad behaviour, however, needs to be discussed.
- If some of the criticism is warranted, speak to your children when the grandfather is not around. Agree on more acceptable behaviour.
- If the criticism is not justified and your father is just being his cantankerous self, don't let yourself be sidetracked by his counter challenge. You *are* the children's mother, you *are* an adult, and you have a right to defend your children.
- In a quiet moment, without the children around, tell your father that he is spoiling the family Sundays with his negative attitude and that you want him to make every effort to stop his criticizing or he won't be welcome any more.
- Stick to your guns. If he is trying to sidetrack again, agree with him. 'I may be a bad mother, but I still don't want you to criticize my children all the time.' Use the time honoured 'broken record' method by repeating your request again and again until it has sunk in. If this does not seem to work, ask him to take out some Sundays to think about it rather than come and visit you.

Women in particular often feel that it is their duty to allow hurtful remarks and behaviour from their parents because of their seniority ('She is my mother after all!'). This is an unconstructive attitude. As long as you allow a certain behaviour, whether it is in your children, your parents, your partner or your boss, they are getting the message that this behaviour is OK, and they will continue. Unless you are a secret masochist who enjoys being hurt and upset by others, it is your responsibility towards yourself to stop others from misbehaving. *This includes your parents.* Erica's children have no way of defending themselves except for disappearing when the grandfather arrives. It seems hardly fair to force the children to either endure the grandfather's rantings or to have to leave the house, just to indulge a self-righteous old man. He needs to understand that his negative attitude will not be tolerated, and if he cannot make more of an effort to be pleasant, he forfeits his Sundays with his family.

EMOTIONAL BLACKMAIL

Emotional blackmail is a special form of manipulation which appeals to your feelings of compassion and duty to make you do things you don't really want to do, or to stop you from doing things you want to do. The reasons behind emotional blackmail are always of a selfish nature, even though, paradoxically, the word 'selfish' is often used to exert the emotional blackmail in the first place.

EXAMPLE
Sandra (35) has been looking after her mother ever since her father died 18 months ago. Before he died, Sandra had spent over half a year helping her mother care for her bedridden father. The death of her husband had distressed Sandra's mother so much that she was very depressed for a long time, and Sandra had spent all her free time, including her weekends, with her mother, which meant a car journey of over two hours each way to get to her mother's house. Sandra had practically no time to herself, and her social life had disappeared altogether. After two years of commuting every weekend Sandra was exhausted but reluctant to curtail the time she spent comforting her mother. Whenever she suggested that maybe they skipped a weekend, her mother seemed to encourage her, but somehow managed at the same time to convey her

disappointment about her daughter's proposed absence. She would say something like, 'You go right ahead dear, I'm sure I'll find something to do' or 'It will be really lonely without you' or 'You are all I've got now.' And Sandra would shelve her weekend plans and get on her way to her mother's . . .

Even though Sandra's mother did not call her daughter 'selfish' directly, she was certainly implying it, suggesting that she would be lonely, bored or unhappy if Sandra didn't come up for the weekend. The mother *says* she understands that Sandra wants to have time to herself, but she immediately goes and overrides her statement by pointing to her own needs, knowing that her dutiful daughter will always end up putting her mother's needs before her own. Compared to the mother's unhappiness, the daughter's wish to have her own life pales into insignificance as far as the mother is concerned. She makes it look practically frivolous that Sandra wants to see her friends. The message the mother is giving is 'I'm old, frail and bereaved. I need your company. You have all the time in the world to see your friends when I'm gone.' This is not what the mother says though. She only hints at her age ('God knows how much longer I'll be around now that dad has gone') or at her need for company ('I'll find something to do'), but it is enough to trigger a feeling of guilt that is sufficiently strong to deter Sandra from doing what she wants to do. Sandra wants to be a good daughter, and if that means giving up her personal happiness then that's what she has to do. Her feelings of guilt are stronger than her sense of self-preservation; her compassion for her mother's apparent suffering greater than that for her own misery.

But compliance over a long period of time takes its toll. Even though the mother managed to tie Sandra to her by appealing to her sense of compassion, Sandra began to grow resentful. At the same time, she felt guilty ('She is an old lady and she is still so fragile after dad's death!' and 'I shouldn't mind going to see her; after all, she has nobody else!'). Sandra was trying to shove her own needs to the back of her mind, but after a while it affected her mood. She was physically exhausted by the drive to her mother's after a demanding week at work, and she was getting tired of listening to her mother going over the same old stories. Her mother got invitations from neighbours and friends but regularly declined them because she did not feel up to seeing other people. Instead, she spent hours lamenting to Sandra about the loss of her husband ('I'll never be happy again without Ed.') Sandra realized with alarm that she had obviously been elected to step into her father's shoes and take over the task of making her mother happy, and that this appeared to be a job for life.

Sandra originally came for help when she had put on three stone in weight and was unable to lose it. In her sessions, it turned out that she had been so busy consoling her mother that she herself had never had time to grieve. Because she always appeared to be the strong one, no one had ever encouraged her to speak about her feelings. When this finally happened in one of her sessions, she felt a lot better, but she still over-ate until she became more confident and resolved the situation with her mother without feeling guilty any more.

When you are in a situation where someone is manipulating you directly or indirectly by appealing to your sense of duty or by trying to make you feel guilty, consider the following solutions.

- Use the Screen Exercise 1 (p.82) to get an outsider's point of view of the existing situation. Check carefully who is getting things their own way. Who is really the selfish person?
- If you find it difficult to disengage yourself from the events on the screen, put a friend into your place on the screen.
- Check how you feel about the emotional blackmailer.
- Once you have done the exercise, notice what is happening with your feelings of guilt as you now think about your own situation.

- Use the Future Projection Exercises 1 and 2 (p.78) to check where you want to go in life and contrast it with where you actually will be going unless you tackle the current problems.
- Next time you meet the person in question, be polite, be friendly, but stand by your plan. Be firm when you say what you want to do. In Sandra's case, she learnt to say, 'Mum, next week I won't be coming up' rather than 'Mum, I was thinking of maybe staying at home next weekend. What do you think?' Say what you are going to do; don't ask.
- Make it a rule to only react to direct requests. Choose to overlook or not hear any indirect hints.
- If the other person shows a moody reaction, confirm this openly but stand by what you said. 'I'm sorry if my wanting to have some time to myself puts you into a bad mood, but I would still like to spend next weekend at home.'
- Stay polite. If you are getting a reaction which is unacceptable, take your leave and let them know that you will contact them later. It can be useful to drop that person a line to say you are sorry they took things so hard, but that they are welcome to contact you when they feel less upset. However, *do not apologize for what you wanted!*
- If you need to speak to the person in question over the phone and you anticipate emotional blackmail, write down your key sentence on a piece of paper which you put next to the phone. That way you are reminded of what it is you want. In Sandra's case that could be 'I have decided to stay home next weekend.'
- Be helpful by suggesting alternatives. Sandra encouraged her mother to ask a friend of the family over for tea, and to accept more of the invitations that were being extended from neighbours.
- Once you have offered some alternatives, it is up to the other person to follow them up.
- Remember that it is your responsibility to look after your

needs, but it is not your responsibility to make another person happy. It is right to be helpful; it is a waste to sacrifice your life.

In most cases, dealing kindly but firmly with an emotional blackmailer will sort out matters, and as long as you keep up a more determined stance, you can considerably improve your relationship with the other person. It is amazing how the fact that you respect yourself more rubs off onto others. It is only when people finally stand up to be counted that they receive better treatment from their friends, family and people at work.

However, some seasoned emotional vampires won't let go quite yet, even when you are firm. There are a few more tricks they might use once you are past the first hurdle. It is important that you bear in mind that emotional blackmail is employed to make you back off from what you want, so don't be impressed by any of the following.

- Once you have said what you are going to do, the other person withdraws, sulks, becomes monosyllabic or looks at you like a wounded deer for the rest of the day. The aim is to make you feel sorry for them, or guilty for having upset them.

  Counteract by acknowledging that they are upset, but re-affirm that you are still going to do what you said ('I can see that you're upset, and I wish you weren't, but I still don't want you to open my mail.').
- Some people will try and change the subject when they feel you are criticizing them ('There are more important issues.').

  Counteract by not allowing them to avoid the issue ('It is important to me that we should discuss my work performance now.').
- Another tried and tested distraction technique is to ridicule you for raising the issue, implying that you are over-reacting, hysterical or unreasonable. This reaction can

easily make you very angry, so do everything in your power to *keep calm.*

Counteract by agreeing with them, but still insist on what you asked for ('You may well think that this is an over-reaction, but I still want you to be more civil to my friends.').

If you can keep cool throughout the other person's manoeuvring, you will win eventually. It is true that some manipulative people can bring you close to blowing your top, only to tell you that you are getting worked up over nothing. But even if you burst into tears, you should still repeat what it is you want.

OUTSIDE DISAPPROVAL

Pressure to remain in the duty trap can be exerted by the person who is at the receiving end of your dutiful ministrations, or it can come, often quite unexpectedly, from the outside. Neighbours, friends of the family, relatives and even members of the immediate family who have long since moved out and lead their own lives will often advise, criticize or condemn from afar. They judge your behaviour according to what they think is wrong or right, and they treat you accordingly. Some of them will come straight out with their opinion and tell you off ('Your poor old dad, sitting there all by himself! Why don't you come over more often?'); others talk behind your back about your lack of consideration for your elderly parents, and yet others give you the cold shoulder when you meet them. None of these situations is very pleasant.

Outside disapproval is usually expressed when it appears that you are unwilling to take on a duty in the first place, or when you show signs of abandoning your duty. Somehow all those people who would never dream of offering to help now emerge from the woodwork and tell you that you should be ashamed of yourself. On challenging them by pointing out that they could contribute by visiting your parents more often, they usually have an excuse ready. If you are single, and especially if you are a single daughter, you will be told that you are the natural choice because you don't have a family. It is often in the interest of other siblings to keep the single sister firmly in place because once she diminishes her efforts or even gives up her duties, they may be called upon to help. In order to avoid the sister relinquishing her efforts, either flattery or the threat of disapproval are employed, both of which are manipulative methods which play on the sister's emotions. Statements like 'Nobody handles mother as well as you do' or 'You are definitely dad's favourite, he kept asking about you all the time we were there!' are designed to give you a sense of importance and indispensability which makes it harder for you to back out of your duties; it would be quite unforgivable for the favourite child to let down the parents.

The reason why children neglect their parents when they are old is often rooted in the past. Unfinished business can survive for decades, and can determine how children react to their parents later on in life. Usually the hatchet is buried once the children have grown up. The parents have mellowed, the children view the parents' behaviour with more compassion, and the fact that you don't have to live under one roof any more does the rest to dispel animosity. But some parents don't change, and some children cannot forget. If a childhood is governed by fear, lack of warmth and absence of understanding, the child is unable to build a good rapport with the parents. Having felt neglected or not accepted in childhood, no foundations are laid for a caring attitude towards the parents once they are old. In many cases, the children of such parents will still stay in touch because they feel sorry seeing the parents frail and powerless, but others will stay away because the parents are no more than strangers to them.

No outsider can know about this past because it is normally not spoken about. This means that anyone else's assessment of the situation is only as valid as their understanding of the family history.

EXAMPLE
Ian (42) lived at home with his parents until he started university. During his last years at home, his family took in his mother's mother who was widowed and not in the best of health, although she was not bedridden. Ian remembers his grandmother as a sweet old lady who helped around the house. He also remembers his mother being very disdainful of his grandmother whenever she made a little mistake such as putting some cutlery away into the wrong drawer. Ian's mother treated the grandmother harshly, ignored her frequently and made her feel like a nuisance. At the time, Ian was appalled by his mother's rudeness. Years later he found out that the grandmother had been a very harsh woman when she was younger, beating her daughter terribly for any minor misbehaviour and locking her into the coal cellar for hours on end where the child suffered the most dreadful fears.

When even members of the family don't know, how can outsiders really understand the dynamics that govern a family? What do outsiders know about the goings-on behind closed doors? The old lady who is so charming when she speaks to her neighbour may be anything but charming to her children when they visit. How often are we surprised at a marriage splitting up because we considered it to be an ideal relationship, only to find out later that she had affairs, or he was a gambler.

It has to be said, though, that in some people the fear of outside disapproval is exaggerated and mainly a reflection of their own insecurity. If you lack confidence and self-esteem, other people and what they think of you gets elevated to an unjustifiably high position. You feel that you are judged (always negatively) every step of the way. You feel you have to justify everything you do, especially if it deviates from *what you think others think* is right and proper. Following your own feelings and honouring some of your own needs becomes too risky even to contemplate. If others criticized you for doing so, it would shatter the last bit of self-respect you have and you would be devastated.

Unconfident people assume that they know what others are thinking about them. Their expectation to be criticized reflects their underlying belief of unworthiness, so that they are not just held back by any real or imagined outside disapproval, but also by their own inability to take themselves seriously.

And yet once you have become aware of your own unease about carrying out a particular task, you embark on a train of thought that will ultimately require you to make a decision. Notwithstanding whether you are confident or not, it can be difficult to distinguish whether you abandon a task for selfish reasons, or whether your motives are valid and it is acceptable to withdraw.

EXAMPLE
Suzanne (35) is a single woman who has spent several years building up her own business after deciding at the age of 30 that she was not made to work for other people. She has always worked long hours, but spends most of her free time with her widowed mother who has started showing signs of senility over the last twelve months. On one occasion, Suzanne found a saucepan on the cooker with the contents burnt to a black mass, with the ring still on; at other times, her mother addressed her as 'Pauline', confusing Suzanne with her long-dead aunt, or did not recognize her at all for a while. It was clear to Suzanne that it was no longer safe for her mother to be at home on her own. On the other hand, Suzanne was agonizing over the fact that her mother wouldn't understand, and would therefore be very upset if she was moved from the house she had lived in all her life

to an old people's home where everything would be new for her.

Suzanne could not decide whether a move to a home would be really best for her mother, or whether she was only wanting to move her because it would make her own life easier. She was worried that she might be seen as an uncaring person who got rid of her old mother once things became difficult. Some of her mother's neighbours suggested Suzanne move back home to keep an eye on her mother, but that would have been a full-time job which would have meant Suzanne giving up her business. She felt that whatever decision she made would be wrong.

Sometimes, the right thing to do is also the most obvious thing to do. Suzanne's spontaneous reaction when her mother's mental deterioration had become obvious was to get her to a safe place where she would be well looked after. She had known from the first what had to be done, but it was her fear of being judged callous or indifferent that made her hesitate, waiting for direction or even permission from others.

The situation was finally resolved when Suzanne realized that this permission would never be forthcoming and that she was the only person who could make a decision. She understood that if the decision lay with her, judgement of that decision rested with her as well, and not with others. She realized that it made no sense for her to give up her business and look after her mother instead as this would leave her financially destitute. She also stopped agonizing about upsetting her mother by moving her when she admitted to herself that a lot of the time her mother did not understand what was happening even while she was in her own home.

Suzanne finally found a small home with kind and dedicated staff where her mother had company throughout the day if she wanted, and where optional activities gave structure to her day.

If you feel that you are held back from making a decision by your fear of outside disapproval, consider the following:

- Other people can never know what it is like to be in your particular situation because they are only looking on and not living it every day.
- Other people cannot correctly assess your situation because they do not have all the necessary information. This means that they cannot possibly advise you about what you should do.
- *You* are in the situation, *you* need to decide; no one can do it for you.
- You are the only person qualified to *make* a decision which means that you are also the only person qualified to *judge* that decision.

THE SAVIOUR SYNDROME

Devotion to another person is not always what it seems. Giving another person your full attention and pandering to their every need can be a sign of love, especially when this devotion is reciprocated by the other person to a similar extent. Where, however, the deference is strictly one-sided, the motivation behind it may be something other than love.

One reason why people display great zeal in pleasing another person is because they feel guilty about something (or because they are being made to feel so), and indulging the other person is a way of atoning for the wrong they have done. Examples for this behaviour can often be found between parents and children, with frequently absent fathers showering the children with presents, or divorced mothers abandoning all attempts at guiding and controlling their children's behaviour because they feel so guilty for having subjected the children to the trauma of a family split-up.

Another reason for dedicating yourself so exclusively to a partner or relative with a problem is because you over-estimate what you can do to help them. The belief that you can save your partner from their drug or alcohol problem, their depressions or their jealousies often makes the problem worse. While you can agonize and sympathize, you cannot really do anything to help your partner. It takes a professional therapist to do that job, but above all it takes your partner *to want to overcome his or her affliction.* Once they get the necessary professional help, it makes sense for you to give them moral support. As long as they don't seek outside assistance, you won't be able to save them, no matter what you think or what your partner tells you.

EXAMPLE
Richard's marriage was definitely over as far as he could see. He (48) and Janet (40) had been to marriage guidance sessions, but the truth was that there was no love left. They had met when they both had their own motives for needing to get married, but those reasons had changed over the years, and they were not compatible enough to enjoy each other's company any more. In the last three years of their five-year marriage, they hadn't had sex, and now they hardly spoke to one another unless it concerned their daughter Charlotte (8).

Richard wanted desperately to get out of the marriage, but at the same time he was very concerned about the effects of a split-up on his young daughter. His marriage was unbearably bleak, and he felt that if he stayed in it any longer he would go crazy, but if he decided to give in to his own needs, he might do emotional damage to Charlotte who he adored.

In the end, he decided to ask Janet for a divorce, and when they finally separated, Charlotte was indeed distraught. Both parents tried to explain matters to her, but the child remained upset for a long time afterwards. Richard felt very guilty for his decision to see to his own needs, and consequently he spoilt Charlotte whenever he had a chance. He let her get away with all kinds of bad behaviour because he considered it just punishment for having deserted her. Charlotte became quite wilful, and soon learned to play off one parent against the other. She was disruptive at school, aggressive towards other children and would ignore what her teachers told her. Richard, in his guilt, was very understanding of all of Charlotte's misdemeanours and explained them as consequences of the trauma the child had suffered through the divorce. He kept on indulging her to make up for what he considered his selfishness, and Charlotte kept on misbehaving.

Ideally, when a marriage ends it does so amicably, and partners go on to establish independent lives whilst they still both take responsibility for the wellbeing of their children. In a perfect world, the partner who has left stays in close contact with the children, turns up regularly to take them out and sends them presents for their birthdays and Christmas so that the children escape the family split-up without being too traumatized. Unfortunately, this ideal is rarely accomplished. More often than not strong feelings lead to discord and rows, and everybody involved, including the in-laws, are upset and confused by the divorce.

In our example, Richard feels guilty for having subjected his young daughter to the ordeal of divorce, and he is trying to save her from the consequences of trauma by removing all boundaries – he lets her do whatever she wants. He feels that he has already burdened his child enough; he does not want to make it worse by making demands on her behaviour. He is afraid that his daughter will hate him for going away, so he does everything *he thinks she wants*. He buys her sweets and presents, takes her out to places he hopes will entertain her, and generally lifts all restrictions. But instead of being happier, Charlotte feels more insecure without her guidelines. If the divorce has upset her, the lack of guidance makes it worse. By removing all boundaries, Richard is abdicating his responsibilities as a parent and leaving it to the child to direct her own life, hoping she will love him for the freedom he gives her.

Yet how absurd to expect a child to cope with that sort

of freedom! Children depend on adults to teach them how to cope with life, how to solve problems in a constructive manner and how to become independent people who can function adequately within society. Instead, Charlotte learns a different lesson. She begins to understand that it is OK to misbehave if you are upset. Not only will you not be punished, you even get some extra treats from your father, so why should she bother with her teachers' reprimands or her mother's entreaties? Charlotte was soon classified as a 'difficult' child who was dreaded by teachers and shunned by other children. She became more isolated, more frustrated and more aggressive, and treated her indulgent father with contempt.

Richard had to learn to let go of his guilt about the divorce and to re-accept his role as an adult who is in charge of his child's upbringing. He began to understand that there are better ways of showing his love to his daughter and that he could help Charlotte overcome the family split-up by speaking to her about it, and by reassuring her that the divorce had not occurred because of anything she had done. This latter statement turned out to be of great importance to Charlotte. Richard found out that she had somehow felt it was all her fault, and this was part of the reason that had prompted her to misbehave at school in the first place. With Richard's revised approach, his relationship with Charlotte improved significantly, as did her performance and conduct at school.

Love that is driven by guilt is a damaging thing because it obscures your vision. When you devote yourself to someone out of a sense of guilt, you no longer see the other person in a rational light. You engulf them with affection and attention without checking whether you give them what they really need, or whether you are heaping onto them emotions that are meant to make them grateful to you so that you can feel absolved from your guilt.

Bear in mind the following:

• Just because you give someone else something that is a

sacrifice for you does not mean the other person has to be grateful.

• Just because you have made a special effort for someone else does not mean that you have done the right thing for them.

• Devotion that is driven by guilt is not the same thing as love – love is free, devotion is love in shackles.

• Telling the other person directly that you are sorry your actions have upset them is a better way of dealing with your guilt than years of trying to make up for it indirectly.

Guilt and a feeling of inadequacy can also be a contributory factor to problems between two adults. When a person has problems with substance addiction or suffers from severe emotional problems, their partner is often faced with a difficult choice. Should they overlook the problem or should they address it? Maybe it is just a passing phase which will blow over soon?

When you first become aware that your partner or a member of your family has an addiction or a severe emotional problem, it is understandable that initially you are hoping for it to go away by itself. It is still useful, though, to mention to the person in question that you have noticed that, for example, they seem to be down a lot of the time or that they seem to drink more. The answer you get in response to your statement can be an indication of how matters stand. Someone who is still quite together will either acknowledge that your statement is accurate, or at least ask you why you think so. Someone who is beginning to lose control over their problem is more likely to deny that there is a problem at all. If, in spite of denials, the problem patently continues, this can be very upsetting for those close to that person. Watching someone you love in distress is a terrible thing, and naturally you will want to help them by being there for them and by being supportive. When your attempts to help fail, professional help is required, but not everyone can accept this. Some people will try even harder, feeling they have failed their partner unless they try again and again to help them overcome their problem.

EXAMPLE

Max (36) had been going out with Danielle (27) for three years. Generally, the relationship was very good, but Max was concerned about Danielle's drinking. They tended to go out fairly regularly with their friends, mostly to pubs and wine bars. All went well for the first six months, but gradually problems began to arise on their evenings out. Max liked his drink, and so did Danielle, only Danielle did not know when to stop. She drank until she was bleary-eyed, and once she reached this stage, she became loud and aggressive, not just towards Max but also with their friends, insulting them and sometimes using foul language. Initially, these unpleasant scenes happened only occasionally, but gradually Danielle seemed to lose control more and more easily under the influence of alcohol.

Right from the start, Max addressed the problem with Danielle. He sat her down and asked her what she remembered of the previous evening. She admitted recalling a few things she had said, but not all of it. When Max filled in the gaps, she would not believe him at first. Only when another friend confirmed that she had made the insulting remarks did Danielle apologize, both to Max and the person she had insulted. She was a bit quiet for a few days, and promised Max that it would never happen again.

All went well for a few weeks. Danielle pulled herself together, but gradually she slipped back into her old behaviour. Max was very angry with her and she was remorseful. She kept promising that it wouldn't happen again, but by this stage Max didn't believe her and insisted she get some professional help for her problem. Tearfully, Danielle promised to do so and attended a couple of sessions with a therapist, but then dropped out. Max refused to take her to any more evenings out because her behaviour had already resulted in him losing a couple of friends. Danielle promised again to go back to therapy, but broke it off after only one session.

Max felt in a quandary. He found Danielle's behaviour quite unacceptable, but it was obvious that she needed help. He decided to stand by her. He talked to her about her excessive drinking, but she would not listen. She accused him of nagging and of exaggerating the problem and maintained that if he wasn't over-reacting as he did, she would not feel the need to drink. Max felt confused, helpless and angry. On several occasions he told her he wanted to move out, but she got so upset, pleading with him to stay, that he always ended up unpacking his case again.

When Max began to look at his own attitudes and feelings concerning Danielle, he described to me the great sense of responsibility he felt for her. He believed that Danielle's happiness lay in his hands only because she had told him so again and again. Sometimes she threatened she would kill herself if he left her, sometimes she would accuse him of making it impossible for her to get better because she lived in constant fear that he might walk out on her, and this stress drove her to drink. She maintained that if only Max stayed with her, everything would be alright and she would be able to relax and be happy.

Max felt overwhelmed by the burden that Danielle placed on him, but at the same time he believed her. He thought that the only way to save Danielle from her unhappiness and her drink problem was to sacrifice his own wishes and needs and stay with her. At the same time he knew that he could not really help her, but Danielle kept contradicting him. So Max ended up confused and frustrated, but unable to leave. Had he overlooked something? Had he omitted to do something for Danielle that would help her? Was it his inadequacy that stopped her from getting better?

It took Max quite a few sessions of psychotherapy to begin to understand that his sacrifice was in vain. By staying with Danielle, he did not help her at all but stopped her taking responsibility for her condition. If he wanted to give her a chance, he had to insist she went to a clinic to dry out, and if she was unwilling to do so, he needed to leave. If he didn't leave her, both of them would eventually be destroyed. If he left, she would be forced to face the options and make her own choice, which would be her responsibility, and hers alone.

For many addicts, the way up can only start once they have hit rock bottom. As long as they have someone around to whom they can hand the burden of responsibility, they will. They declare someone else their saviour and they are often very convincing.

Check whether you are with someone who makes you think of any of the following.

- I'm the only person who understands him/her.
- I can't leave him/her *now*.
- I'd rather stay and put up with his/her problem than leave and have to cope with my guilty conscience.
- If only I tried harder, I'm sure I could help him/her more.
- It's probably something I've done in the past that has given him/her the problem in the first place, so I can't just bail out of my responsibilities now.
- I'm the only one he/she will listen to; a therapist couldn't get through to him/her.

If you suspect that you might have bought into the role of 'saviour', do the Future Projection Exercises 1 and 2 (p.78–9) to get back a sense of direction. It is also useful to go through the first Screen Exercise (p.82) to detach yourself from present events and gain a more unemotional assessment of what is happening in your life at the moment. In addition, ask yourself the following question.

- What will happen with you if you continue to play the 'saviour' for another year/two years/three years?

How demoralized are you now? Could you take it for another year, or would you expect to break down under the burden? If you feel that you could collapse mentally or physically, you need to make a change to your situation *now*. If you won't make a decision, life will make that decision for you.

> Max decided that he had to stay with Danielle. She did not make any efforts to deal with her alcohol problem, and their relationship deteriorated steadily. Max finally had a nervous breakdown which caused him to lose his job. Danielle, who had always maintained she couldn't live without him, went off with someone else who was also an alcoholic. Max ended up with his health in tatters, without a job and the belated realization that he had not, after all, been able to save Danielle.

If you feel that you cannot extricate yourself from a damaging relationship because you hold yourself responsible for the other person's condition, consider the following points:

- Are you only staying because you feel you couldn't cope with the feelings of guilt if you went?
- Are you concentrating on your partner's problems to avoid having to look at your own?
- Do you have silent rages against your partner which you cannot express constructively because you are afraid of him/her, or because you fear his/her reactions?

If you answer 'yes' to any of the above questions you should seek professional help yourself. Get your own problems sorted out and build up your self-confidence so you can feel more in control. This will make it easier for you to deal with your difficult partner in a way that is constructive for both of you.

12

Negotiating With Integrity

THE MOST popular useless method of dealing with problems is not to speak about them in the hope that they will go away by themselves. So great is the fear of potential unpleasantness that people will often choose passivity and suffering rather than activity and solution. What stops people from taking positive action is the assumption that asking for what you want automatically involves conflict and arguments, and is therefore by definition an unpleasant affair.

It is true that when two people have differing expectations of one another, emotions are involved, and that can make it more difficult to discuss the problem sensibly. However, there are techniques that can help you keep your emotions under wraps, and we shall look at several ways of doing so in this section of the book. There is a lot you can do to improve your circumstances and the way other people behave towards you, but you have to be willing to speak about your problems.

Once you have established a habit of tackling problems head-on, in a constructive way, it is quite amazing what can be achieved. Any lack of success in solving unsatisfactory situations usually results from a lack of constructive attempts to do so. Because people don't know how to negotiate, they don't get results, and then they give up because they believe that there is no way out of their difficult situation.

Negotiating a better deal for yourself can be a rewarding experience, not only for you, but also for the person you negotiate with. Once a grievance has been aired in an appropriate manner, the relationship between the two parties concerned will, in the majority of cases, improve dramatically. When, however, negotiations are conducted in an aggressive or insensitive manner, arguments can ensue which make it less likely that the other person will be willing to discuss the situation with you on another occasion. This is why it is so important to prepare yourself well, and to understand how to conduct yourself within the negotiation set-up.

THE BASICS OF NEGOTIATING

Before you can sit down with the other party to start negotiating, you will have to do some homework. You have to get yourself into the right frame of mind and establish some clear inner guidelines to allow you to stay on track once you have started the process. The clearer you are about your objectives and the particular stance you wish to take when you speak to the other person, the greater your chances of success.

There are some common mistakes that people make when they contemplate addressing a difficult issue, and any of these can result in an unsatisfactory outcome.

Mistake No. 1 – Not knowing what you want

There is not much point in calling a meeting if you don't have an agenda, so make sure that you have thought through carefully *beforehand* what you want the outcome to be. Determine the following for yourself:

• What would be the *ideal* outcome?

- What would be a *realistic* outcome?
- What is the minimum of concessions that you need from the other person to feel the meeting was worth your while?

Establishing answers to these three questions is important not only because it helps you stay focused during negotiations, but also because you need to be prepared to display some flexibility in your approach, otherwise you may end up just bulldozing over the other person's needs and feelings.

EXAMPLE
Rosemary wants her two brothers to help look after their ageing parents by visiting them. Both brothers have their own families, as does Rosemary.

Ideal outcome: The three siblings take turns in visiting the parents instead of Rosemary doing it all the time.
Realistic outcome: The brothers commit themselves to visiting the parents every three months.
Minimum outcome: The brothers commit themselves to speaking to the parents on the phone once a month and to visit them twice a year.

You can see in this example that the outcomes are clearly defined. Rather than saying 'more often', the objective is 'once every three months' or 'twice a year'. 'More often' is too vague and therefore often easily pushed aside and forgotten.

Mistake No. 2 – Blaming and manipulating

There may be a great temptation to do to others as you feel they have done to you. The person you plan to speak to may be the world's greatest critic or manipulator, but that still doesn't make these methods of interaction acceptable. When you negotiate, bear in mind the following:

- Treat your negotiation with the other person as a professional matter, regardless of whether you are dealing with your parent, child, friend, neighbour or work colleague. Be firm and clear.
- Prepare to speak about facts, not opinions. It is OK to speak about your feelings; it is not a good idea to use them to persuade someone else to comply with what you want.
- Trying to get someone else to change their ways by blaming them is more likely to end up in them withdrawing than in greater co-operation.

EXAMPLE

Alex has a colleague, Hazel, whose sloppy performance at work has caused numerous problems in the past. Alex is quite annoyed at her disregard of other people's deadlines, but he also understands that he must keep his emotions in check when he speaks to Hazel. In his meeting with her, he plans to point out the discrepancies between what she *says* she will do and what she ends up actually doing. He realizes that he needs to be professional in his approach, rather than emotional or personal, if he wants better co-operation from her.

Mistake No. 3 – Not appreciating the other person's reasons and feelings

Just because you feel your needs have not been taken into consideration by the other party this should not be taken as a licence to ignore their needs and feelings. Besides, it can be of benefit for both sides to ascertain the motivation behind certain behaviours. Once you understand *why* someone is acting in a particular manner, it becomes possible to negotiate better ways of achieving the same aim.

Remember:

- By respecting the other person's needs, you make it more likely that they will show consideration for yours, so make sure you find out the reason behind their unacceptable behaviour.
- Always make sure that you also juxtapose what *your* needs are and *your* reasons behind your reaction. Appreciating someone else's situation does not mean that you have to ignore your own. The whole point of negotiating is to find a balance between your needs and those of the other party. You are not set on a take-over bid; you are engaged in promoting a successful merger, where everyone feels they have gained something.

EXAMPLE
Becky and her teenage daughter, Amanda, are at logger-heads over Amanda's refusal to help at home. Rather than continuing to have rows over this issue, Becky decides to sit down with Amanda and find out what the problem is really all about. Becky refrains from pointing out that Ralph, Amanda's brother, is much more helpful around the house than Amanda. It turns out that Amanda is quite prepared to help, but finds that Becky won't let her do it at a more convenient time. Mother and daughter agree on what Amanda considers to be a better time of day, and Becky stops pushing Amanda to do things immediately. As a result there are now far less rows, and on the whole Amanda is more helpful than ever before.

Mistake No. 4 – Lecturing and psychoanalyzing

When you are a participant in a negotiation, you need to start from the premise that, on a human level, you are the same as the person you are negotiating with, even if that person is younger or less experienced than you. By lecturing or psychoanalyzing them, you give yourself an air of superiority which is bound to evoke irritation. The whole point of a negotiation is to resolve a problematic situation; it is not to put someone else in their place or to display your intellectual skills.

- Don't squander an opportunity to negotiate by making it into an ego-boosting session for yourself. Your view of the problem or your view of the other person may not be based on sufficient information to make it reliable. This is why it is wiser not to pretend from the outset that you know everything there is to know about the problem. You might find it more helpful to *ask* the other person what the reasons behind their actions are.

- If you want to be taken seriously, you have to be prepared to listen to the other person, in a way that is not blocked by your own preconceptions of him or her. Long speeches on your part prevent you from gleaning new information which could help solve the problem.

EXAMPLE
Whenever Edward came home, there was trouble. He had hardly closed the front door when his wife Melissa bombarded him with her woes about the children, what they had done wrong and how they hadn't done what they were expected to. Edward was convinced that Melissa was simply too soft with the boys, and all that was needed was more firmness. 'After all, they are not playing up when they're with *me*!' He then launched into a long speech about how it was all Melissa's fault, stating that she would never be any good as a mother until she learned to assert herself with the children. He went on until she cried, and then he patted her on the back and thought to himself that it was a shame that she was such a weak person . . .

Without checking, Edward assumes he knows where the

problem lies: namely with his wife's lack of authority. As it turned out later, two of his boys were being bullied at school and consequently became aggressive at home. But Melissa is also making a mistake in the way she is tackling the problem, and that is:

Mistake No. 5 – Opening negotiations without composure

Always, always, always simmer down before you open negotiations. It is no wonder Edward thinks Melissa is weak, because that is the picture she presents when he gets home. She seems in a permanent state of panic which makes it more difficult to treat her like an adult.

- Don't enter negotiations whilst you are confused about what you want, or are angry, panicky or upset.
- Don't negotiate anything while you are both standing up and in a hurry. Make sure you can speak in private and that there is enough time available to discuss matters to the full.
- Switch off the radio, television and any other sources of distraction.
- Agree on a convenient time with the other person. Do not impose a particular time. 'If this matter is not important enough for you to discuss now, we might as well leave it!' is not acceptable, but it is OK to let the other person know that you expect them to give you their choice of time within the next day or two.

It may not always be easy or possible to *keep* your composure during negotiations, but at least you can make sure that you start off in a calm and collected manner. If the problem concerns a domestic matter, it may seem easier to be more casual about *when* you will sit down and talk and *where* you are going to do so. However, your chances of bringing the negotiations to a mutually satisfactory conclusion are greater when you plan them properly and give them 100 per cent of your attention, as you would if something needs sorting out at work.

THOROUGH PREPARATION IS HALF THE BATTLE

Most people feel apprehensive when it comes to bargaining for better conditions for themselves. One reason for these feelings of trepidation lies in the fact that it is impossible to predict how the other party will react to your request for change. There is always the inherent risk of being rejected or ridiculed which means that you may make yourself vulnerable by initiating the negotiation process.

On the other hand, the big advantage of being the first to set the ball rolling is that it gives you greater control because you can prepare yourself. Being well prepared gives you confidence, and that in itself will make it easier for you to come across as calm and collected during the negotiation process.

In the following, you will find four essential steps which you should take before you approach the other person to suggest a meeting. It won't take you too long to conclude these preparations, but make sure you don't rush them. Take some time out to think matters through, sleep on it, and if you still feel that you have come to the right conclusions the next day, arrange for a meeting with the other person.

Get your facts straight

You feel that you have worked very hard for the other person, putting in time and effort to make sure they are all right and that they have everything they need. At the same time, you do not feel that your efforts are being appreciated.

- Is this really true, though? Check very carefully whether the other person is in fact showing their appreciation, but in a different way from what you expected. Be fair and give the other person credit where they deserve it. In the majority of cases, people are thoughtless rather than malicious.

- Jot down what it is they do that makes you feel bad, adding at least two examples of when you observed this unacceptable behaviour. Only use examples where you feel they behaved badly towards *you*, even though you may have noticed them doing the same thing to someone else. Stick to your own experience, and don't base your negotiations on hearsay; this is not relevant to your preparations. For your upcoming negotiation, stick to matters that concern *your* relationship with your partner-in-negotiation.

- Once you have completed your list, see if you can find a common denominator. For example, you may have written down:

    My wife/boss puts me down in front of others.
    She never says thank you, even when I have put myself out for her.
    She frequently interrupts me when I'm speaking.

In these examples, the common denominator would be 'rudeness'. If you are not sure whether you are over-reacting or whether the other person is indeed rude, imagine yourself treating someone else in this way. This little exercise will make it clear very quickly whether you have grounds to complain or not.

Constructive phrasing

Think carefully how you can put your complaint to the other person in such a way that it leaves their dignity intact and allows them to apologize if they wish. Remember that you are not going to get the results you want unless you allow the negotiation channel to remain open.

Constructive phrasing for the above list may sound as follows:

'I find it very hurtful/it really upsets me/I don't find it acceptable when you put me down in front of others *as you did when the Johnsons were over last week.*'

Combine your constructive phrasing with one, maximum two, concrete examples of when the offensive behaviour occurred.

- Practise putting your case by saying your constructive phrasing out loud several times in an even and measured tone of voice. This will help the words come out more easily on the day. And no matter how strong the urge is to dramatize, withstand it at all cost! Avoid emotive language; stick to the facts.
- Find a positive opener for your constructive phrasing. If at all possible, find something positive to say about the other person *before* you go into your complaint. If your wife has a good sense of humour, but often uses it to put you down in public, mention this.

'One of the things I really like about you is your sense of humour, but sometimes I feel you are going a bit too far. I find it really hurtful when you put me down in front of others as you did when the Johnsons were over last week.'

In a professional context, phrase the positive opener slightly differently.

'I have always had a high regard for your management skills/knowledge, but . . .'

'I appreciate the fact that you have been so helpful to me in the past. I wonder whether you could help me sort out another matter. I was quite disconcerted the other day when . . .'

However, *do not lie*. If there is nothing positive to say about the other person, do not invent something or it will eventually backfire. Only say what you really believe to be true.

Find a general opener for your negotiation. A useful phrase is:

> 'I've got a problem, and I wonder whether you could help me with it.'

This is non-aggressive and non-accusatory, and therefore a good neutral introduction.

What outcome do you want?

If you don't know where you are going, you can't get lost, but you will also never arrive. You need to be clear what end result you want before you can put it to anyone else.

- Determine what the ideal outcome would be and to what degree you would be willing to compromise, without feeling that you have come away with nothing from the negotiation.

  In most cases, this is quite a straightforward process. You are likely to want the other person to stop doing a particular thing, or to start doing another. During the preparatory stage, it is advisable to be as clearcut as possible, otherwise you end up with indistinct boundaries which are no good in the actual negotiation.

- Determine what you want the other person to do so that your outcome can be achieved. If, for example, your boyfriend expects you to cook supper every night, there is no point in just telling him he is lazy or selfish. You need to tell him what you want him to do, which can be either to take over the cooking every other day, buy a take-away for the two of you or treat you to meals out over the weekend in compensation for you doing the cooking during the week.

  You can see that in thinking about what you want the other person to do, you can already start looking for a variety of options that both of you might find acceptable.

Anticipate reactions

Hopefully, the actual negotiation will be going according to plan, but it is always a good idea to prepare yourself for any negative reactions that threaten to throw the negotiating process out of kilter. Have some options ready in case that happens.

- The other person might get upset and start crying. Be prepared to keep calm and ask them *why* they are upset. Tears can denote a variety of feelings, so don't assume that you know what they mean, and above all don't apologize immediately and withdraw your complaint; otherwise your partner's tears will have been in vain and your problem remains unsolved.
- The other person might be unwilling to change his behaviour. If this is the case, do not back off. Ask them to suggest a solution that would take care of your needs as well as their own. If no satisfactory resolution is reached, ask him to have another think about the matter and agree a time to reconvene. Stand firm by your statement that this is a *real* problem for you, and that you expect it to be taken seriously.

Once you have concluded the preparation stage, it is time to call your meeting. Make sure that you plan for enough time and that the meeting place affords privacy. When you ask the other person for a meeting, don't get drawn into a discussion about the problem. Say that you can't discuss it now or that you are in a hurry, fix the day and time and then disappear.

HANDLING YOURSELF DURING NEGOTIATIONS

So now you have prepared yourself, and the time has come to actually sit down and talk to the other person. Make sure you *both* sit down, and that radio, television or any computers in the room are switched off. If possible, sit at an angle to the other person rather than directly opposite them. This positioning will make your talk less formal, and it also allows you and the other person to avoid looking at one another if you don't want to. This can be helpful when either of you finds it difficult to speak about something during negotiations. Some people find constant eye contact aggressive or challenging, and this may set the wrong tone for your conversation. If you are both comfortable with frequent eye contact, you can still have that while sitting at an angle to one another.

Opening the conversation

Start off with your prepared opener without dragging it out; get to the point straight away. That way, you will get it over and done with more quickly and you won't annoy the other person by leaving them suspended for too long. Finish off by posing a question, such as, 'What can we do about this?' Once you have posed this question, *do not say anything at all*. Wait.

Some people find it hard to pause and not fill in the gap, but this is essential in negotiations, not only because you need to demonstrate that you can listen, but also to keep your cool. Too much verbiage can result in you talking yourself into anger or into tears, and this can stop you from getting your message across.

Listen very carefully to what the other person is saying. You may not get the answer you expected, but that does not mean that it is all going wrong. As there are always different ways of resolving a problem, consider the answer you are getting as one of several options and give it due consideration. Allow the other person to explain how they would implement the solution. *Let them finish what they are saying* even if you can already see that it wouldn't work for you.

Whenever Vicky's brother Steve needs any help, he summons Vicky. Steve and his wife Janet are moving house and have already included Vicky in their list of volunteer helpers. Steve and Janet have just had their first baby and automatically expect Vicky to babysit for them so they can go out, even though Vicky is married and working. So far, Vicky has obliged, but she is becoming increasingly resentful at being taken for granted. When she speaks to Steve about it, he suggests that he won't enlist Vicky's help in future, but Vicky explains that this is not the issue. She does not mind helping but she wants to be *asked* so she has an opportunity to say yes or no, depending on how much time she has.

Other people cannot read your mind. It is up to you to let them know if they get something wrong. This is the only way you can make sure they can get it right the next time. Some people are insensitive to other people's boundaries, and as long as you go along with them, you are deemed to be consenting. Even though you are under no obligation to consent, you nevertheless have a responsibility towards yourself to clarify the matter with the person concerned.

Understanding one another

Before you get to a final answer, you may want to find out why the other person was acting as they did.

Rita's mother rang her every night and kept her on the phone for a long time. Rita, who had a demanding job, found these regular calls intrusive and asked her mother not to ring so often, but her mother continued. When Rita finally sat down with her mother and talked it through, it turned out that her mother had felt panicky on two occasions over the last months, both times in the evenings, and had since then been very afraid of the panic attacks recurring. By ringing her daughter, she was less afraid because she felt she was not on her own. She hadn't told Rita about her panic attacks because she didn't want to worry her.

In the case of Rita's mother, there is a very good reason for the disruptive behaviour. The advantage of having found out about it is that now Rita can help her mother do something constructive about her panic attacks, such as seeing a counsellor or a hypnotherapist. Tackling the problem together will also result in the bonus of mother and daughter getting closer. Something that started as a discord can end up making a relationship better than it has ever been.

In other cases, the reason that is given for unacceptable behaviour is that someone was over-reacting to what was meant to be only a joke. A wife who puts her husband down in front of friends may indeed not be serious about what she says, but this does not make her put-downs any less hurtful. If the wife can only display her wit at her husband's expense, she is not being funny: she is on an ego trip. So when you are being told that you are making a mountain out of a molehill, don't backpedal. 'I may lack a sense of humour, but I still don't want you to put me down in front of others.' Remember – the best way of keeping the focus on the main issue is by stating what you want repeatedly. Do not allow yourself to be sidetracked into discussions that lead away from your request. You may or may not be a sensitive person, but that does not alter the fact that you have the right to request that your sensitivity be taken into account.

Being nice is not the answer

In negotiations there may be a temptation to make concessions too easily, especially when you feel a sense of relief that the other person is willing to negotiate with you. You may want to demonstrate that you are a nice person, and women in particular tend to make that mistake. However, negotiations are not about being nice, they are about resolving issues, so be professional about it. You do not have to be rude, heartless or hard as nails to do a good job in a negotiation, but you need to stick to the issue, repeat if necessary what it is you want and make it clear if you feel that the two of you have not yet arrived at a satisfactory solution.

EXAMPLE

Charlotte feels discontented because her boyfriend Greg has been making some major decisions without consulting her. Whether it is where to go for their annual holiday, or having the living room recarpeted, Greg makes the arrangements, puts down the deposit and *then* tells Charlotte about it. As Greg always pays for these things, he seems to feel entitled to make the decisions without checking with Charlotte. Charlotte, who is earning money herself and would not mind contributing towards these purchases, is disgruntled even though she generally likes what Greg decides. When Charlotte finally speaks to him, he is very willing to listen, but is ultimately unable to understand why Charlotte wants things to change if she *likes* what he is buying. Charlotte begins to have doubts about the legitimacy of her request. Greg is so kind and generous, so why does she have to be so critical? She agrees with Greg that maybe this wasn't really such an important issue after all, and leaves it at that. The conversation leaves her dissatisfied.

What Greg is saying makes a lot of sense from his point of view. Why does Charlotte complain when she likes what he buys? The problem in this case is that Charlotte has not thought thoroughly enough *why* it bothers her what Greg is doing. After a conversation with her friend, Charlotte realizes that it makes her feel unequal in the relationship when she is not allowed to be part of the decision-making process and to contribute financially to those purchases. She goes back and explains this to Greg who still doesn't understand ('But I don't mind paying for it, and if you like it, what's the problem?') but promises to involve Charlotte from now on.

Finalizing matters

Before you both get up from the negotiating table, make sure the other person understands what it is you want them to do. Check that you have expressed yourself in an unambiguous way, and ask the other person for their consent to trying out a different approach. Say, 'When we go to the party on Saturday, can we please implement our agreement that you won't make any jokes about me?' or 'Next time you want to buy something for the house, will you please ask me?' or 'Next time you want to have a chat with me, will you please make sure it is before 10pm?'

When the issue under discussion is a complex one, you may want to agree on a provisional plan of action which can be tried out over a few weeks or months. In this case, it makes sense to set a date where you can review the situation and make any further adjustments should that prove necessary.

EXAMPLE

Tony is married to Alexandra; they have no children. Alexandra is a high-flyer and very involved in her job, which means she often works long hours. Tony feels that their relationship is suffering because they are spending less and less time together. Somehow, Alexandra's job has become the Number One in her life and Tony feels left out. When he raises the issue with Alexandra, she confirms that this is so, but says that she feels she has no choice if she wants to succeed. They agree on making at least three hours time once a week where they do something together. Alexandra promises to keep that time clear in her diary and that they will review the situation in a month's time.

Once you have come to an agreement, thank the other person for having given you the opportunity to discuss matters. It can also be a good idea to ask whether the other person wants to raise any issues concerning yourself, although in most cases this will transpire during negotiations.

Many people find that they can take a more lighthearted view of the issue under discussion once a solution has been negotiated.

EXAMPLE

Sonja was exasperated by Claudia who kept ringing up and wanting to go out. They had met at a workshop and had made friends, but whereas Claudia was retired, Sonja was very busy running her own business. Sonja was dismayed that Claudia seemed unable to understand that she did not have that much spare time on her hands. Even though Sonja had said a few times that she felt hassled by Claudia's phone calls, nothing changed. Finally, Sonja decided to write to Claudia to say she wanted to break off contact. Claudia was very upset when she received the letter and asked Sonja for a meeting. Once matters were clarified, the relationship improved. Claudia left it to Sonja to ring her when she wanted to meet up, and they both could make good-natured jokes about Sonja's need not to be crowded. Sonja now felt free to ring Claudia occasionally just for a chat, without having to fear the dreaded question of when they could get together again, and their meetings became happier and more enjoyable.

Even though it may not always be possible to come to a mutually agreeable solution, you will be surprised at how often you can be successful, even if you are not perfect at negotiating.

If no satisfactory agreement can be reached, or if agreed solutions are not adhered to by the other party, you may want to consider parting company. In a work situation, this can mean speaking to someone at a higher level or, if this fails to bring the desired results, to look for another job. For a personal relationship, this can mean breaking off contact temporarily or permanently, moving out or ending the relationship. Thankfully, it is rarely necessary to go this far, but where there are no other options left, you need to be prepared to take that step. It is important though not to use these last measures as a threat during negotiations, especially if you don't really mean it. Your bluff might be called, or the other person might feel bulldozed into consenting when they don't really want to. This may result in a short-term 'victory' for you, but it is unlikely that the other person will keep to their promise for very long since it was given under duress.

WHEN YOU SHOULD THINK TWICE BEFORE NEGOTIATING

Even though negotiation is a very effective tool to help you escape the duty trap, there are a few situations where you should think twice about offering to talk. Look at the following list and answer 'yes' or 'no' to each statement.

The person you consider negotiating with:

- has in the past displayed a violent temper;
- has been known to physically attack others;
- has in the past threatened to physically harm you or your children;
- has a drink or drug problem;
- has episodes of mental illness;
- has in the past made your life unbearable if he or she suspected you of disagreeing with them;
- has used negotiations in the past to belittle or ridicule you;
- has repeatedly disregarded agreements made in earlier negotiations.

Clearly, every time you answer 'yes' to an item on this list, and
even if you only answered 'yes' once, negotiation is unlikely
to be the best course of action. No doubt every human being
deserves a chance in life, and most people also deserve a second
chance. However, when you or your children are in danger of
being harmed, you need to put safety first. If you have evidence
that an attempt to negotiate will provoke violence, you need
to get out fast, no matter how convincingly the other person
promises to mend their ways. Unfortunately, there is not much
point in holding your negotiation in a public place or in the
presence of a friend, hoping that this will make it less likely
that your partner will blow a fuse – if you have to go home with
him afterwards, or your friend leaves, you are still unsafe.

Equally, if you have attempted in the past to have a serious
talk with the other person and were unable to get their
co-operation, your relationship is in all likelihood doomed.
With every time you try again, and with every subsequent
failure, you lose more self-respect. Most people know when
it is time to draw the consequences, but the fear of being
on their own or, when it is a professional situation, the
worry of being unemployed, together with a misplaced sense
of loyalty, stops them from detaching themselves from the
harmful relationship.

EXAMPLE
Henry is a successful executive on a high salary which allows
him to provide his family with a very comfortable life style.
He has lived with Harriet for eight years and they have two
children. Henry is a 'Jekyll-and-Hyde' personality. He can
be devastatingly charming to his wife, especially in public,
but more often than not he can be cold and even violent.
He is very critical, and when things at home are not to his
satisfaction, he has been known to pin Harriet against the
wall, scream at her and spit in her face, as well as throwing
her down the stairs. His mood swings are unpredictable.
After an attack, he will give her a superb bunch of flowers

or take her out for a grand meal and, with that, considers the whole matter forgotten. Meanwhile, Harriet has lost all confidence and has started believing that she is useless. Maybe if she just tried *harder* . . .

Of course Harriet will never be able to get it right. When she finally realized this she left, taking the children with her. Only then did Henry admit to himself that he had a problem and began a course of therapy sessions. At the same time, he kept ringing her up, alternately cajoling her to take him back or threatening her. He accused her of breaking up their relationship and depriving their children of their father. Harriet felt guilty because it was true that it had been *her* who had decided to walk out. Had she just been selfish? Should she have stuck it out for the children's sake? Did her duty lie with her partner or with her children?

When there is violence in a relationship, even if it is just verbal, it is essential you make every effort to remove yourself and your children from that environment. The children may well miss their father, and if he has never harmed them, it can be arranged that he can see them, but the trauma of hearing and seeing their mother being mistreated is far more damaging to the children in the long run than a divorce or separation.

Depending on how bad the situation is at home, you may or may not want to discuss matters with your partner. If you feel you can risk it to negotiate, you should certainly make sure that you have a contingency plan in case he gets violent. This means asking some friends to stand by in case you need to move out there and then, or making arrangements so you (and the children, if you have any) have somewhere to stay for at least a few days. This is one of the few situations where it can be wise *not* to communicate, but to move out while your partner is away from the house, just leaving a note on the kitchen table.

13

VALUES FOR THE 21ST CENTURY

SO WHERE do we go from here? Where can the growing trend for self-fulfilment and self-actualization lead as we cross the threshold into a new century?

The 20th century has seen enormous progress in many areas. Women are much closer to equality than they were at the beginning of the century, progress on the race issue has been made in many countries, human rights are being defended more vigorously now than ever before, and with therapy and personal growth courses increasingly accepted and more widely available, the welfare and personal development of the individual has become the centre of attention, especially over the last thirty years. Some claim that this has resulted in people becoming more selfish, with everyone fending for themselves and only looking after number one. This, however, is contradicted by the great number of charitable organizations who look after those in need. We are obviously prepared to give money to help others, but is this just an underhand way of abdicating our responsibility to charities to care for those we do not want or cannot be bothered to look after ourselves?

The fact is that society has changed considerably over the last hundred years. Family structures have changed, as have jobs, education and the ways in which we relate to one another. Moral codes have been stripped of many taboos which, on the one hand, has provided us with more freedom but, at the same time, deprives us of a supportive structure which used to act as a guideline for the individual. It is now much harder to know for sure what is right and what is wrong. Today, our personal responsibilities are far greater than they ever were because we have this abundance of choice which is no longer limited by social conventions. This new freedom can be frightening, even paralyzing, because admitting that you have a choice, that you can make a decision about what to do with your life and how to live it, means that you become accountable for the outcome.

The release from old social conventions and taboos finally allows us to look at our personal feelings and needs. Therapy and personal growth groups can help us recognize, accept and verbalize our needs so that we can find constructive ways of fulfilling them without forgetting that this has to happen in a way that respects the presence of others. Theoretically, we are a big step further on in our personal development, but on a practical level many people still find it difficult to verbalize their needs. Although they can recognize how their relationships with others have to change, they are still too riddled with guilt to initiate that process. No doubt part of the problem is to be found in the individual's personality and background history, but an additional factor is that we have become somewhat paranoid of being biased or subjective. This trend towards non-committal, non-judgemental attitudes becomes particularly obvious in the way we speak.

In today's politically correct world, the boundaries between right and wrong have become severely blurred through the way we use language. In an attempt to stay objective and to avoid discrimination, we can no longer say what we mean. When social services describe a wife-beater as displaying 'inappropriate behaviour', this in no way describes adequately the fact that the wife ended up in hospital with a fractured nose and several broken ribs. The term 'inappropriate behaviour' is a euphemism which is misleading, but above all it is a way of using language that allows neither the public nor the perpetrator to distinguish between physical assault and a *faux pas* at table. If you blow your nose on the tablecloth, now *that* is inappropriate behaviour . . .

Of course there have to be shades of grey between the extremes of right and wrong, but at the same time we have to beware of a growing tendency to care more about the perpetrator than the victim. It is laudable that a greater understanding of the impact of upbringing, social environment and circumstances has led to fairer judgements in the law courts. This means that a person who kills someone after having been abused by them for years is more likely today than twenty years ago to receive a lenient sentence. Human actions are no longer viewed as black or white, and this is a good thing. The disadvantage is that, at times, this results in a loss of direction. It is clearly desirable to make the police force accountable for their actions, but a law that prevents a policeman from grabbing a young thief by the arm for fear of being accused of assault helps no one.

Somewhere along the line we seem to have lost touch with common sense. It appears that the pendulum has swung from one extreme to another. Whereas at one time society condemned anyone who was different because being different was already a crime, we now seem to feel that we have to 'understand' and consequently tolerate all manner of hurtful or damaging behaviour unless we want to be regarded as reactionary. Where common sense would dictate a clear statement, political correctness demands neutral socio-babble which blurs boundaries and no longer encourages the individual to take responsibility for his or her actions.

In order to interact successfully with others, we need meaningful language, and this has to be used in constructive ways to inform, communicate and develop the self. And yet there is less and less emphasis on the competent use of language. People spend a great deal of time sitting in front of television, video and computer screens, at work as well as at home. Mealtimes are no longer an opportunity for the family to get together and speak to one another because both parents are working, and the children lead their own lives from an early age. On the whole we seem to spend more time 'communicating' with machines than speaking to real people, with families glued to the television set for hours and computer games replacing human interaction. As human relationships are being neglected, the world on the screen becomes more 'real' than the real world.

Technology is useful, but it cannot and should not replace human interaction or we will end up emotionally dissatisfied. Consuming mental junk food leaves us empty, and today's growing drug culture shows that we are well on our way to a spiritual desert. We are becoming richer on the outside and poorer on the inside.

If we want to halt this trend, we need to get back to a successful togetherness with everyone around us. The foundation stones for a happy and meaningful life have not really changed since the beginning of mankind. We want to feel successful, we want to be wanted and we want to get a kick out of walking this earth. Without relating to others, we will never truly achieve any of these aims.

To interrelate successfully, we have to learn to communicate more openly and more frequently, and we have to learn to negotiate rather than fight for what we want. Hate comes from feeling deprived; love grows when you are satisfied and safe. Not all of us have had the luxury of a happy childhood with parents who could teach us the essential life skills, but most of us have the ability to learn how to change things for the better. Communication can be learned. With every person who learns to communicate, with every person who is committed to making their relationships with others work better, there is one more person in the world who can love. You can only give when you have. Self-development is one step on the way to a better future.

Useful Addresses

UK

Counselling/psychotherapy

Metanoia
13 North Common Road
London W5 2QB

British Association of Psychotherapy
121 Hendon Lane
London N3 3PS

Hypnotherapy

The Corporation of Advanced Hypnotherapy
PO Box 70
Southport
Merseyside PR8 3JB

The London School of Eclectic Hypnotherapy
808A High Road
Finchley
London N12 9QU

Positive Thinking

The Peiffer Foundation
39 Minniedale
Surbiton
Surrey KT5 8DH

USA

American Society of Clinical Hypnosis (ASCH)
Suite 291
2200 East Devon Avenue
Des Plaines, IL
600118–4534

Society for Clinical and Experimental Hypnosis (SCEH)
6728 Old McLean
Village Road
McLean, VA 22101

Australia

Australian Society of Hypnosis
Secretary: Dr Mark Earl
Austin Hospital
Heidelberg, Victoria 3084

For further information, Vera can be contacted at
The Peiffer Foundation
39 Minniedale
Surbiton
Surrey KT5 8DH
Tel: 020 8404 9774
E-mail: positive@blueyonder.co.uk

INDEX